John Haughton

Char-ee-kar and Service There with the 4th Goorkha Regiment in 1841

An Episode of the First Afghan War

John Haughton

Char-ee-kar and Service There with the 4th Goorkha Regiment in 1841
An Episode of the First Afghan War

ISBN/EAN: 9783337778682

Printed in Europe, USA, Canada, Australia, Japan

Cover: Foto ©ninafisch / pixelio.de

More available books at **www.hansebooks.com**

CHAR-EE-KAR

AND

SERVICE THERE WITH THE

4TH GOORKHA REGIMENT

(SHAH SHOOJA'S FORCE),

IN 1841;

AN EPISODE OF THE

FIRST AFGHAN WAR

BY

COLONEL HAUGHTON, C.S.I.

———————

LONDON :
PROVOST AND CO., 40, TAVISTOCK STREET,
COVENT GARDEN.
1879.

PREFACE.

It will be remembered by some who read this account that, on my return to England after the close of the Afghan Campaign in 1843, I was earnestly requested by them to publish a narrative of the events I witnessed, or in which I took part during that Campaign. It is desirable, therefore, to record the reasons which induced me to abstain from doing so then ; as also those by which I have been influenced, after the lapse of a generation, in compiling the statements here prefaced. Several narratives, some especially referring to the disastrous period of the campaign, have been published. One in particular, Eyre's Journal, contained an account of the defence of Char-ee-kar from the pen of my friend and companion, Major Eldred Pottinger, written while he was still held a prisoner by the Afghans ; it contained some expressions which, had I been at the writer's elbow, he would doubtless have altered ; but it was sent home for publication before we met. On the whole, it was a fair account ; though from the fact that the writer of it was wounded, while acting as a volunteer with the Native Artillery, within a few hours of his taking refuge with our garrison, and confined to his bed till we were about to retreat, it was impossible he could be perfectly informed of all that took place at that time. I was not ambitious of parading my name before the public, and I knew very well that if I wrote a full and true account, with such comments as I should then have felt bound to make, if writing for public information, I should hurt the feelings of the friends of many deceased brother officers, raise a nest of hornets about my own ears, and enter an arena of literary strife, for which I was unsuited by habit and inclination. For these reasons I remained silent. Since then, from time to time, writers who had occasion to refer to Char-ee kar, have frequently made the mistake of attributing the defence of that post to Eldred Pottinger ; but this has generally occurred in a way which I could only meet publicly by a lengthy narrative, and on one notable occasion by appearing to side with my gallant comrade's enemies. I have more than once privately remonstrated, and received promise of justice, as usual in such cases, to be meted out to me at a future time. Last year Mr. Kaye, in his memoir of Pottinger, published I think in *Good Words*, again alluded to Eldred Pottinger as the defender of Char-ee-kar. I went to him to point out his error, and at his suggestion drew up the accompanying memoir, to be made use of in correcting his next edition of the *War in Afghanistan*. While writing, I had occasion for geographical information, on a trivial point, on which my memory was at variance with Pottinger's published account; I applied to Mr. Kaye to obtain access to a map, believed to be alone accessible through his or some other official's favour. That gentleman never replied to my note. I have concluded, therefore, that it must have been consigned to his "Balaam Box," with that of the Emperor of Abyssinia—distinguished company, no doubt. The result is that (unlike the Emperor, having no opportunity of making reprisals), the labour of my pen goes to my private friends, instead of having the honour of furnishing material for the historian. I have recently had access to a MS. Map in the Surveyor General's Office, Calcutta, which proves that my memory of the geography of the country is correct.

In compiling this, I have referred to Eyre's Journal; to an account published in the *Englishman* Newspaper in 1842 by Major McSherry, from dictation of Moteeram Havildar* of the Goorkha Regiment; and to a memorandum written by myself at the time, the last ever penned with my right hand.

My friend, Colonel Reid, R.A., has obligingly altered Moteeram's sketch in accordance with my memory; but it makes the place look more imposing than it really was. The extract of Major Robert Codrington's letter, in the appendix, more correctly describes the weakness of the position.

In conclusion, I must add that I have not the least desire to detract in any way from the high reputation of Major Pottinger, nobly earned. It will be seen from the narrative that to his chivalrous refusal to abandon me, I owe my life when wounded; but I wish to make plain that to Captain Christopher Codrington, and to myself after his death, the credit is due of having, as Commander of the Goorkha Regiment, defended the post of Char-ee-kar. Pottinger's own letter in the appendix ought, I think, to settle this, were it *disputed*, which in reality has not as yet been the case.

I have one more remark to make. Eldred Pottinger, in writing his narrative, naturally spoke of what had been done, as any one present would do: "We advanced," "we retreated," are natural expressions; but the use of the pronoun generally is not intended to convey the idea that the

*See appendix.

writer advanced or ordered an advance or retreat, but denotes the act of the writer's party. So when Pottinger says it was owing to my conduct that "we were able to hold out," it cannot be inferred that he meant to convey the idea that he was the commandant of the place ; there are similar expressions in his published narrative, and I am not in the least surprised that, in the absence of anything from my own pen, casual readers were under the impression that Pottinger commanded at Char-ee-kar. I remember well that a portion of the English public imbibed the belief, from the frequent mention of her son-in-law by Lady Sale, that he was the chief defender of Kabool.

I have placed in the appendix the statements of two survivors of the garrison, unexpectedly met with since the narrative was penned, and also the printed narrative of Motee Ram Havildar. Numerous discrepancies may be observed ; but memory is frail, and not to be much depended upon in such exciting times. Had I been questioned immediately on arrival in Kabool, I could not have said how long our siege had lasted—it was one very long day to me. The circumstances I have stated have induced me to write of Char-ee-kar ; perhaps, if ever leisure permits, I may pen adventures during the campaign, earlier and later.

PREFACE OF THE SECOND EDITION.

This pamphlet is reprinted almost verbatim from the edition privately circulated in 1867. I am now moved to publish it by the fact that the narrative by the late Major Eldred Pottinger, C.B., of the same event has been recently reprinted—verbatim, I believe—and consequently liable to the same mis-interpretation as the original was. The appendices are given more with a view of showing that my statements are not exaggerated, than as being correct narratives of facts. Indeed, of two of the writers—Moteeram and Mohun Beer—it can only be said that their narratives, however interesting, contain much that is erroneous and confusing. My own account was made use of by Lieutenant Low (of late) I.N., in an article published by him in *Every Boy's Magazine*, in 1877.

CHAR-EE-KAR.

In the year 1839 the powers ruling India sent Shah Shooja-ool-Moolk to his native country, accompanied by an army composed of English and Indian troops, to secure his restoration to the throne of Afghanistan, from which he had been expelled thirty years previously, and which he had often since in vain tried to regain. I believe the original project was to seat him on his throne, and then leave him to his own resources, with the aid only of a small contingent of Indian troops, to be raised, officered, and drilled by officers detached from the armies of India. The plan did not prove successful, for, contrary to the expectation entertained, it became apparent that, however unpopular the former Ruler, Dost Mohamed, might have been, Shah Shooja was not a whit less so. Some did not at all yield submission to him, and as early as the spring of 1840 there was a serious rebellion, also put down by English troops, in what is called the Kohistan; and altogether it was found that Shah Shooja could not get on without their assistance. We had garrisons at Kabool, at Ghuznee, at Kelat-ee-Giljee, at Kandahar, and also at Quetta, at the head of the Bolan Pass. The troops raised specially for the Shah's service were scattered about, and acted in conjunction with the others. The Kohistan, which General Sale had with much difficulty brought into order in the latter end of 1840, was thought to require the presence of troops to keep the inhabitants in awe; and a very small Regiment was raised for the purpose and stationed at Char-ee-kar, the principal town of the district, under command of Lieutenant Maule, of the Bengal Artillery. The Kohistan had a native Governor; but a Political Officer, with an Assistant, and a Doctor to attend to their health, were stationed in it also, with what view I know not. Early in 1841 the Native Corps raised specially for the purpose was deemed insufficient for "overawing" the inhabitants, and a Regiment of the Shah's Indian troops, composed of Goorkhas, chiefly natives of Nepaul, was sent to take its place. These were further supported by two six and one eighteen-pounder guns, manned by some of the Shah's own gunners (Mahomedans, natives of the Punjab), under the nominal command of an eunuch of the seraglio, who, however, did not leave his more delicate charge. Thus much has been said to show that the country, the scene of this narrative, was chronically in an insubordinate state. Dost Mahomed himself had only been able to master it by an act of notable treachery, so his country-men reported. It is said that, under security of a solemn oath, he invited all the chiefs to a conference, and then murdered them. All the male inhabitants were used to arms, and usually carried them. In fact, it was an ordinary sight to see men at the plough with swords by their sides and matchlock and shield slung at their backs.

The whole of Afghanistan is mountainous; it is, therefore, not easy to say why the country to the north of Kabool and south of the great range separating Kabool from Turkistan, should be called the " Kohistan," or Hill Country; but such is the fact. There is a high range of mountains shutting in the valley of Kohistan to the west, another to the north and east; and two low ranges of hills lie between it and Kabool. The valley varies in width, but is nowhere less than twelve miles wide. Although a large river, in many places unfordable, runs through the valley, collecting the waters of numerous streams, the general character of the valley is dry and sterile, cultivation being generally con-fined to the gorges and immediate foot of the mountains, as the soil, from its nature, does not retain water, and can only be cul-tivated where the supply is abundant. To be sure, some canals for the purpose of irrigation exist, but the turbulent character of the people is unfavourable to works of this sort, involving, as they do, much labour, and so easy of destruction as they are.

The inhabitants are for the most part located in castles, the walls of which are formed of mud, very solid, and able to resist the fire of small ordnance. Every landholder, or at least every family of any respectability, had one of these, and even in the towns of Char-ee-kar and Istalif there were several.

There were no wells in the country, the nature of the subsoil, containing (as it did) huge boulders, prohibiting it. The inhabi-tants were, therefore, dependent for water upon streams issuing

from the mountains, or canals from them. These canals were
generally lined with gardens and mulberry trees, and, on one
side at least, had a band of cultivation beyond.

Char-ee-kar was reckoned to be about forty miles, as the crow
flies, from Kabool. It contained a population of, perhaps, three
thousand inhabitants, and derived its supply of water from a
canal which conveyed the waters of the river of Ghorebund.
The head of the canal was said to be distant nine or ten miles.
The town was situated at the termination of the slope of the
western hills, from which it was distant about two miles. The
canal from Ghorebund and the road to Kabool ran parallel to the
mountains for some miles, dividing the cultivated country from
the mountain slope almost devoid of vegetation. It was on this
slope, close to the town of Char-ee-kar, that the Goorkha
Regiment was stationed.

By ascending the slope a short distance, we could see into
Nijrow, Gain, Bala Gain, and Doornama valleys on the opposite
side of the great one, and distant from fifteen to twenty miles,
which had either never submitted or speedily thrown off the
yoke of Shah Shooja.

Amid the cultivation, not far removed from the canal, and
about three miles distant from Char-ee-kar in the direction of
Kabool, were a cluster of castles called Lughmanee. I believe
they were the forfeited property of some native chief. There was
located Major Pottinger, C.B., the Political Agent, who had
earned a name throughout Europe and Central Asia by his
defence of Herat. With him were Lieutenant Rattray, his
assistant, and the Doctor; he had numerous Afghan retainers,
and a guard of Goorkhas from Char-ee-kar.

The Goorkha Regiment of Shah Shooja's Force was sent to
Char-ee-kar in the month of April or May, 1841, to take the place
of the Kohistanee Regiment, commanded by Lieutenant Maule.
It is time to begin a more particular account of this corps and its
position The Regiment was raised in 1838 at Lodhiana, in
India, for the service of Shah Shooja. At first it was composed
half of natives of the Himalaya, called Goorkhas, and half of
natives of the plains. However, just before its arrival at Char-
ee-kar it had been remodelled by substituting Goorkha recruits
for the Indians. The great bulk of the Regiment were mere
youths, and fully half had never seen a shot fired. The native
officers and non-commissioned officers were for the most part

very inferior. There were, however, some brilliant exceptions. Most were men who had for many years failed to obtain promotion in the Hill Regiments in India, and had joined Shah Shooja's service to get a step of rank. Somewhat less than one-half of the Regiment had, however, witnessed the capture of Ghuznee, and a portion of them had done good service at Bameean in the previous year. The officers were Captain Codrington, of the 49th Bengal Native Infantry, who commanded it; Lieutenant William Broadfoot, second in command; myself, the Adjutant; Ensign Salusbury, the Quarter-Master; and Ensign Rose, the Subaltern. There were also two European non-commissioned officers, Sergeant-Major Byrne, and Quarter-Master Sergeant Hanrahan. There were about sixteen native commissioned officers, and 742 rank and file. The whole were pretty well drilled, for the Commanding Officer had been himself nine years Adjutant of a Regiment, and added untiring devotion to his duty to a thorough knowledge of it.

When we arrived at Char-ee-kar, we had for months to live in tents; in fact, I occupied a tent up to the time of the outbreak. We found that Lieutenant Maule had commenced Barracks* for his men, which we were to finish and occupy. A square of one hundred yards each way had been enclosed with a mud wall, and it was intended to build rooms against the wall all around for the occupation of the men. The officers' quarters were to be on one side of the enclosure, on the same plan, but of two stories. The houses were to be, like all in the country, flat-roofed. My Commanding Officer and myself were at once struck with the indefensibleness† of the position, and I believe he remonstrated with some one on the subject, though not with the military authorities of the Shah's Force. If he did, nothing came of it. We had to carry on the work after the original plan, and as far as I can remember, the only alteration made was the surreptitious addition of round bastions similiar to those of the native castles. I remember this very clearly, as it was entirely opposed to the instructions Captain Codrington had received, viz., that he was to build merely a Barrack. The sum allowed certainly did not exceed 600l., of which not more than 400l. was expended, a very

---

* See Appendix B.

† In a letter to my father. I described the place as charming, but observed, "I do not understand why we have been sent here, unless the Government are in a hurry to get rid of us."

moderate amount for housing between 900 and* 1,000 souls in
such a climate. It was apparent to us that, in the event of an
attack, water would be a great difficulty, but we were led to
believe that such an event was impossible. However, as, in
addition to my other duties, I had to supervise the building and
keep account of the expenditure, I did reflect very seriously on
the subject of the water supply. We drew that for our ordinary
consumption from the Ghorebund Canal, which passed about one
hundred yards in front of our Barracks, but a very small supply
was also obtainable from Khojeh-seh-Yaran, a little valley in the
hills to the west of us, the proprietor of which allowed the stream
to trickle down once or twice per week to enable us to make
mud for our walls. It occurred to me that we might either
bring this stream down under-ground, or possibly discover
another spring, and so conduct it; for it was palpable that an
open canal above ground might be cut off at any minute. I sent
for the most celebrated diggers of "kahrez," as the underground
conduits are called, who all negatived the possibility of such an
undertaking for the reasons which forbade wells; and, as they
justly observed, had such a measure been practicable, the inhabitants of Char-ee-kar would have resorted to it long since. As
the only other measure we could adopt, we intended that if we
could manage to save enough out of the sum allowed for building the Barracks, we would construct a tank in the centre of the
Barrack-square, which would contain a supply for a few days.
With this view we excavated the earth required for the works
from that spot. It will be seen, however, that this place was
destined to be applied to a very different purpose.

At the time when our trouble commenced, the Barracks were
partially finished. We had four walls, varying from seven to
twenty feet in height, pierced by two gateways, east and west,
with a row of flat-roofed rooms for the men all round the inside,
except at one spot where were the officers' quarters. Unfortunately as yet we had no gate for the eastern entry, or doors for
any of the rooms. The Barrack square was built on a slope, so
that its interior was commanded by the trees bordering the canal
in front, distant about 100 yards. It was also commanded by
the high towers of a castle forming the southern entrance of the
town of Char-ee-kar. Its north, south, and west faces were commanded by a Mahomedan oratory and a butt erected beyond

* Including camp followers, and women and children of the Sepoys.

reach of our muskets. In front, or to the east, the banksof the canal already mentioned, also garden walls, formed abundant shelter for an enemy; but in this direction, what was worst, was a small building beyond the canal, which we ourselves had erected as a mess house, and a stable on the banks of the canal in course of erection for our horses. There were also a low range of mud huts for shelter of our married sepoys; but these were built so as to be pretty well commanded from the Barracks. Any one acquainted with military matters will see that our arrangements were as bad as they well could be. It is to be observed, however, that the slightly defensive character which our Barracks took, was in opposition to the intentions of the ruling authorities. The most rigid economy was the order of the day, and had it been possible to select and make defensible a position (which it certainly was), I feel assured the proposition would have been negatived, and that the proposer would simply have brought himself into disgrace.

We had not been without some indications of the coming storm. Reports of a movement in the adjoining independent districts were rife. Thieves reputed to be from that quarter prowled about; not many days previously a shepherd was killed on the mountains near us, and his flock driven away. Thieves visited our own camp at night. My tent was pitched on the banks of the canal, and I had a guard consisting of a corporal and four privates and a bugler, it being my duty as Adjutant to cause the bugle to be sounded for parade before dawn of day. One man was constantly on sentry, and the rest slept on the ground by him. One night a musket was stolen from beside one of the sleeping sepoys, and on another the bugler's bugle was carried off. These articles were paraded in the independent country. I received a message from an old fakeer to whom I had shown some favour, living at the place called Khojeh-seh-Yaran—the tomb of a saint—recommending me strongly to spend the winter in Kabool; and altogether Codrington and myself believed something wrong was going on. I know that he wrote to this effect either to Major Pottinger or his Assistant, Lieutenant Rattray, and was answered by the latter that he might rest assured of full notice—twenty-four or forty-eight hours' notice, I forget which period was named—of any movement on the part of the rebels in the independent district. Captain Codrington handed me the note, and I put it into my pocket. When

I lay wounded at Kabool, one day an officer came into my room, and seeing a number of papers, the contents of my pocket, lying in a recess of the wall by the side of my bed, said, " What have you got there?" He began to examine the papers, and coming to Rattrays' note, said, " You don't want this; this is of no use to you," and there and then tore it up, and threw it into the fire. I mention this fact as a proof that Captain Codrington was on the alert, and would have been ready to put himself on the defensive if the authorities, under whom he was placed, had encouraged him to do so. The truth to me is plain, that no one in power anticipated any such outbreak as actually took place. All my servants, with one single exception, were Afghans or Persians. One of the latter had recently left me. He was a native of Kandahar, and I have now before me the address he left with me : " Futteh Mahomed, to the care of Khan Mahomed Khan, in the service of Sirdar Poordil Khan;" the latter was one of the brothers of Ameer Dost Mahomed. It is possible that my servant, who refused to give any reason for leaving my service, may have had some inkling of the conspiracy brewing, but I think not. None of the others certainly had any, and they remained faithful to me

Thus much by way of a preliminary. On the morning of the 3rd November, 1841, some of my servants started on business to Kabool. They returned in a few hours, with intimation that the road was occupied by rebels from Nijrow, at a distance of some ten or twelve miles. This was absolutely the first intimation of the existence of any body of rebels in the Shah's territories. After consultation with me, Captain Codrington proceeded at 1 p.m. to communicate this intelligence to Major Pottinger at Lughmanee, and to consult as to what steps should be taken in consequence, Major Pottinger being at that time the officer under whose orders he was acting. What follows, I take from a memorandum now before me, written on the evening of the 4th November, 1841; it is the last I ever wrote with my right hand. It concludes abruptly, for at the time drowsiness rendered me incapable of writing more.

At 2 p.m. firing commenced in the direction of Lughmanee. My first impression was, that it was nothing of importance, and arose out of an attempt of some of the hostage chiefs there detained to make off; but observing that the firing continued and that there were apparently two parties engaged, I deemed it my duty to send to the relief at least of my own commanding officer, who had intended to return immediately, and had evidently been unable to do so. There arose a serious debate in my own mind. Lieutenant William Broadfoot, the second in command, had returned to Kabool to act as Secretary to Sir Alexander Burnes, who was to succeed Sir William Macnaghten. There remained, therefore, only three very junior officers (Ensigns) with the Regiment; I was the senior in years and standing. If I went with the party I proposed to send, I should leave the Regiment—now the most important charge—to the two junior officers. Again, if I sent either of the junior, and any failure took place, men might blame me for not going myself. I concluded that the best plan was to go myself; for, if successful, all was well: if I failed, the attempt would be evidence that I had not left a difficult duty to others. At a quarter to three, therefore, I started with 120 men or thereabouts, in two companies. One great object I had in view was, to get down unobserved, so as to be able to ascertain the actual state of affairs before becoming engaged. Instead, therefore, of following the high road, I at once crossed the canal and marched through the cultivation, thus managing to reach Lughmanee undiscovered. Arrived, I found that the attack was mainly from the Kabool side. I rounded the fort, and then found that the enemy were chiefly occupying a large walled garden, into which I managed to get almost unopposed, one or two men only being wounded. These I was compelled to leave in a ditch, with injunctions to be quite quiet, till the affair was over. The enemy was completely taken by surprise, and at once ran. The entrances to gardens are usually made so small that but one person can enter at a time, and he must bend double to do so. This is done to keep out cattle; thus before the enemy could get out, a good many were killed. The coats (padded with cotton) of several were set on fire by their own gun matches. I mention this, as a similar occurrence has given rise to statements that our troops had burnt the bodies of their enemies.

On our appearance the garrison of Lughmanee also sallied out, and the enemy were driven off at all points. Captain Codrington then strengthened the garrison of Lughmanee to 120 men, and agreed with Major Pottinger to send at dawn next day a supply of provisions and ammunition, which Major Pottinger was to send out a party to receive and convey into his castle. Our entire loss was ten killed and wounded. We got back about sunset; but before I finally joined Captain Codrington, one sad event occurred which troubled him much afterwards. There was a small village adjoining the castles, the principal inhabitants of which came out to assure him of their loyalty, they were unarmed. Unfortunately as he passed, a shot was fired by one of the rebels from the direction of the village. This was attributed to treachery. Our men had, on hearing the report of the rebel shot, prepared to answer it. A raising of the hand and a wave of it, made by my beloved Commander, settled the fate of six elders of the village, who lay dead as I passed. I know only of this fact from his own lips. I have never heard it adverted to since. It is highly probable that these people deserved their fate; for next year, many months after this occurrence, when I was a prisoner in the hands of the Afghans, a young man, to whom I had done a good turn once, was sentry over our party; he formed my acquaintance, and in conversation told me that the little village of Lughmanee lost thirty-three men on that day. We saw nothing of the enemy on our way back to Char-ee-kar by the ordinary road, beyond noting that some still hung about on the road towards Kabool. We reached our barrack after sunset, and made arrangements for our own security, and the supply of provisions and ammunition to be furnished next day. I don't think I slept that night, or took off my clothes then. I know that sleep entirely left me for several weeks after. I only remember once attempting to sleep; it was in the daytime, and was unsuccessful. My usual post at night, when not moving about, was in a chair near the gate, where I soothed my wearied nerves with a cheroot.

Before dawn on the 4th November, the relief promised to Lughmanee was in motion. I started with several ponies, loaded with ammunition and provisions. I had with me my gallant young comrade and dear friend, Ensign Salusbury, Quarter-Master Sergeant Hanrahan, one six-pounder gun, and three weak companies of Goorkhas, or not more than 200 men. There had been heavy firing during the night, so that we knew that the enemy still hung about Lughmanee. It was good broad daylight as we approached, and I observed a considerable body, apparently seven or eight hundred, of the enemy on the slope of the hill to our right, among broken ground; this much embarrassed me. I had the most positive orders not to compromise my party or gun. I was to convoy the stores to what I may call the latitude of Lughmanee, whence, on seeing me, Major Pottinger was to detach a party to receive them. The high road passed Lughmanee at a distance of about 500 yards; by a sharp turn to the left, a narrow lane enclosed by mud walls led to the castle. It was foreseen that if I went down this lane, I might lose my gun and possibly not be able to return. I was cautioned against doing so. I halted and sent Ensign Salusbury and two companies, with orders to turn up the party who threatened our right, and to draw down to my rear if they appeared too much for him, as, when they came out of the broken ground, I should be able to work on them with the gun. The enemy gave way, and our young soldiers pursued them only too precipitately. Bugles were sounded in vain, and orderlies sent out without result. At last, seeing no other means of getting the men back, and observing how the enemy were swarming from all quarters, I sent Sergeant Hanrahan with the greater number of my remaining men to bring them back. All this time I had remained within five hundred yards of Lughmanee, waiting for the people who were to receive the provisions. They came at last—about ten horsemen, who, however, positively refused to return. Circumstances now rendered it impracticable for me to do anything but fall back on Char-ee-kar. When Salusbury rejoined me, the Quarter-Master Sergeant and several of his party were wounded, and the firing had brought together the enemy from all quarters; the whole country seemed alive with them. When we commenced falling back, the men were disposed to bolt altogether, and it was with the greatest difficulty I could save my party by sticking to the gun, and with one or two faithful men loading it and firing it. The enemy's cavalry charged us repeatedly, but as they were compelled to keep to the road, a round from the gun invariably turned them. Before we got over the distance, only three miles, poor Salusbury was mortally wounded, and our numbers much diminished. To wind up, when just within reach of the Barracks, the trail of the gun gave way; but the enemy did not venture to close with us. We at once set about measures for our own defence. What provisions were to be had in the town were brought in; but as the shops and houses were all closed, it was not very easy to get anything, the more so, as we were ignorant of the places in which provisions were stored. One of our first acts was to take posses-

sion of a castle which entirely commanded our Barrack square.
We were anxious to do so with as little offence to the owner as
possible; it was necessary that he should not have the option of
refusing us. Captain Codrington and myself, therefore, went to
the castle, and asked to speak to the owner—Khoja Meer Khan,
I believe, was his name. When he came out, we engaged him
in conversation, while we walked towards our own Barracks. It
was under these rather unfavourable circumstances that I measured the distance, 450 paces. The object we had in view was
civilly explained to him when at the Barrack, and a party of
fifty Goorkhas, under a native officer, was sent over, and took possession without opposition. The owner, indeed,—I believed
then, and do still—was well disposed towards us. The enemy
now hemmed us in on all sides, and we had a day's desultory
fighting; we held, however, full possession of the gardens in
front of our position. They occupied the town, and turned off
the water from the canal; and we at once became dependent for
our supply on what we could obtain from the pools left in it, and
a very small quantity in a pit near the Barracks, from whence
earth had been dug to make bricks.

I gave the armourer directions for the repair of the trail of the
gun, but eventually at night had to work at it with my own
hands. He was no carpenter, though clever in his profession,
and had no idea of the strength required in such a thing as the
trail of a piece of artillery. We examined our ammunition
stores as well as our provisions. Of the latter we had about
seven days' supply, Of the former we had 200 rounds per
musket—less the quantity expended during the previous day.

For the six-pounders we had originally sixty rounds for each,
chiefly of round shot. For the eighteen-pounder we had only
eight round shot and one 24 pound howitzer cannister shot, which
the artillery officer, who sent it out, specially explained, might
" be altered to fit." This is ridiculous enough, but it is fair to
say that the authority who ordered the gun out, only sent it for
show, " for the moral effect." We had a considerable amount of
old lead dug out of the target butt. This was cast into bullets,
and placed in bags made by the tailors and women of the regiment, from the carpets of my tent, to serve in lieu of ordinary
grape and cannister for the six and eighteen-pounders. Later,
when this supply began to run short, we collected all our copper
money, and the nails and fragments of iron in the armourer's

shop, and turned them to the same purpose. They did good service, especially the bullets. Later still, when it was apparent that our bullocks would never be able to drag our gun, the drag chain was cut up into lengths, and bound up for shot. It made very efficient practice among the trees in front, so that the enemy's marksmen dared not occupy them. The chain cut the smaller branches like a knife. The blank musket cartridges, provided for the instruction of recruits, were broken up and formed into cartridges for the great guns.

But to return to our narrative of events. After a hard day we had quiet; and Captain Codrington (who honoured me, as he had always done, with perfect confidence, but on this occasion was pleased specially to approve of my services), desired me to write a report of what had passed, for the information of the military authorities of Shah Shooja's force at Kabool. He added that there was nothing I could write of myself that he would not sign. He had always been in the habit of writing his own letters on public affairs; consequently, for want of practice, writing was irksome to me; of course, I could not have said what he did in my favour in the despatch he subsequently wrote, and which I blushed to read. It was put 'n the post bag destined never to be delivered. I should value this document now more than any honour earthly power could bestow upon me.

After dark, when it was possible to turn our attention from our own immediate affairs to our comrades at Lughmanee, we sent our people in that direction for information. It was not to be expected that under our circumstances people would go unprotected to such a distance as that place; we could gain no tidings —our own people were utterly weary, and had to feed. Excepting the artillerymen, the garrison was composed almost entirely of Hindoos. I do not think that there were more than three Mahomedans in the ranks of the regiment. The Hindoos would not, as a matter of course, eat food cooked by any but themselves or their wives, and, therefore, had fasted all the day. Had they been Mahomedans, one servant might have cooked for a large number, and while toiling and fighting, their food might have been in course of preparation. I strayed out after dark—I think it was about nine o'clock—in the direction of Lughmanee, with only an orderly with me, in the hope that some one might be coming in from that direction. I had not gone far when my quick-sighted companion saw people approaching. We were, of course, prepared for a speedy retreat; but were soon relieved by the discovery that the party consisted of Major Pottinger, the Doctor, their retainers, and our own Sepoys from Lughmanee. Nearly all property had been abandoned. The Doctor had across his shoulders the account book of the Political Agent tied up in a cloth; there were horses, spare guns, etc., but I think no baggage. I quickly escorted them into our quarters, where they were most heartily welcomed by Captain Codrington and Mr. Rose. We all sat down and listened with intense interest to their account of the events which had occurred, and which had induced them to abandon their own place. Our own extreme joy at having them with us was, however, quickly dissipated when we learned the fact that only a portion of our Goorkhas had returned. For several nights I watched that road, in the hope that some more of our men would turn up. They did so as late as two nights after, and my joy was such that, on meeting them, I embraced them, as though they had been my own children. Europeans who have been in India are, perhaps, alone capable of judging of the exuberant feelings by which I must have been actuated, to indulge in such an unwonted demonstration of regard. Yes, I hugged them as though they had been my children. Having thus broken off from my story, I may finish all I have to say about them. They were men stationed on the towers of Major Pottinger's castle, who either did not hear, or did not understand the summons to come down, and who, though the castle was taken, kept their position without food or water till it was deserted by the Afghans, who would not venture to capture them by force, as their position was only accessible by a ladder and through a trap door. It is probable that the interests of the owner of the castle prevented their using fire to expel their enemy.*

Major Pottinger† has himself recorded the details of the defence of Lughmanee.

The 5th November was a sad day for us; we had a most severe struggle for existence, and though entirely successful, had to mourn grievous loss. Early in the morning the enemy mustered to attack us on all sides. It seemed indeed as though the whole male population of the country had assembled against us. I am sure that I am within bounds when I say that on this and several

* It is remarkable that they brought all their property tied on their backs.
† See Eyre's "Journal."

subsequent days, we were besieged by not less than twenty thousand armed men. Had they been at all organized, or under the direction of any man of ability, our destruction was certain. An overruling Providence, however, made their numbers of no avail, and their utmost efforts fruitless. The very excess of their numbers gave us nerve; we also felt quite assured that relief would be sent to us from Kabool when our situation became known; and we felt that the mere interruption of the daily post would cause inquiry, even if Pottinger's messengers sent from Lughmanee§ failed. We had not at this time the most remote suspicion of what had taken place at Kabool. The troops there were in no position to aid us.

On the night of Major Pottinger's arrival a discussion took place between Captain Codrington and myself as to the position of the former, as it appeared not impossible that he might avail himself of his superior military rank to assume command of the garrison, which he had joined. We concluded that by rules of the service he could not do so : that we were still bound to act under his instructions as Political Agent in our intercourse with the natives, but that all military authority would continue with the officers of the regiment. I mention this, as the gallant Major has more than once had the credit of the defence of Char-ee-kar. He did not require this addition to his laurels, and I have proof* under his own hand that he would not have deprived me of it.

The arrangements for the day's defence at its commencement were as follows :—I was sent to command the outpost in front. These were chiefly three walled enclosures, the largest of which contained two or three acres of ground. Pottinger volunteered his services, and was placed in command of the guns; Captain Codrington commanded and supervised the whole.

In the course of the forenoon I received a message from Codrington to the effect that Pottinger was wounded, and requesting me to come to him. Matters were too critical where I was to allow of my leaving. I therefore wrote him an answer,

§ It would seem from Sir W. Macnaghten's unfinished despatch that on the 6th he received a hurried note written by Pottinger from Char-ee-kar. I do not know anything of this, but on the 6th or 7th I think he sent in two Goorkhas unarmed, with a despatch written in invisible ink between the lines of a native manuscript. These men got in safe, survived the campaign, and on my recommendation obtained the Order of Merit.

* Appendix A.

explaining the case, on a piece of cartridge† wrapper with charcoal. Our circumstances were these. The bed of the canal
contained the only supply of water available, a little remaining
in pools here and there. The possession by the enemy of the enclosures I have referred to, would entirely cut us off from this,
and ensure our rapid destruction. It was therefore of vital importance to retain these outposts. While I remained in any one
place, all was safe there; but I was not long absent from any one
position, before the men would gradually drop away, and the
enemy would creep up and gain some advantage. Thus during
the whole day we were engaged in a perpetual struggle to hold
our position. I think it was about noon that I received intelligence of my beloved Commander having fallen, and another summons from him; but it was not till near dusk that I could venture to leave my position. How shall I paint the short interview
which then took place? We were united by the bonds of the most
sincere friendship and mutual esteem. The poor fellow was shot
through the chest and scarce able to speak. He gave me his
watch—which I now wear, but I could not find it, as it had
slipped under him in bed; and when the stern calls of duty compelled me to tear myself from him, he sent a servant after me
with his haversack, containing his telescope and pistols, etc.
with directions to invest me with it. These touching proofs of regard at such a time move me to the heart even after this lapse of
time.

Salusbury, who had been shot through the back on the previous day, had continued in a semi-conscious state, and expired
this afternoon. We kept our posts in spite of the fatigue, caused
by the extreme exertions the men had gone through and the frequent attacks of the enemy during the night.

On the 6th they attacked us with renewed vigour. The possession of the large garden in front was hotly contested, and the
enemy early in the day got possession of it. I was not at
that post at the time, but shortly after, hearing what had
occurred, determined if possible to recapture it. I went up the
bed of the canal, with a few followers, to ascertain the number of
the enemy in possession. I had on the previous day caused
a portion of the wall next to our Barracks to be broken down, but
for its strength I would have destroyed the whole. There was a

---

† By a curious coincidence I met at Buxa, Bootan, since the above was written, an
old sepoy who was with me at Char-ee-kar, and who mentioned this fact to me.

gap about ten feet wide broken down to the height of a man's chest. Up to this I got, and from the silence within thought the place empty. I was soon undeceived, for I found it fully occupied and a sentry standing with his matchlock ready, a pace or two in the rear of the gap: he at once fired at me, but without wounding me. In return I attempted to shoot him with a double barrelled pistol by Staudenmeyer, which, with its fellow, had cost me 30*l*. Both barrels missed fire. I then and there threw both pistols away, and trusted to my sword, the scabbard of which I had lost on the first day of the outbreak. As the enemy at once rushed up to the breach and I had only the Bugle Major with me, of whom more hereafter, I was compelled to take ignobly to my heels; however, the disgrace did not rest long; having collected a sufficient body of men, I easily retook the place. I note here that the enemy never stood when deprived of the protection of walls, even though they were ten to one, or the disproportion was still greater. We could not, however, attack them in the open plain, as our entire number was as nothing to the circle hemming us in. Later in the day I left Serjeant Major Byrne, a gallant soldier, in charge of the post; but shortly after he was brought in mortally wounded I took his place, the Doctor and Mr. Rose defending the Barrack; and the enemy having towards evening retired a little from our outpost, I went out, wishing to see if I could do anything towards the town. I had a very gallant little Goorkha orderly with me, we both kneeled behind the bank of a ditch looking in the direction in which we supposed the enemy to be. We had been in our position but a few minutes, when we were enlightened as to the enemy's "whereabouts." My orderly* was, like most of his race, a little short man, his head and mine were both turned to the left. He was on my left side, a rifle ball passed through his head, striking me on the throat a little to the right side. We both fell : he stone dead, and I feeling paralyzed. I was not at all stunned. Our men, who were watching us, thought both killed; my poor orderly was dragged into the garden as men drag a wheel-barrow, the poor man's legs being used in place of the handles and his back

---

* This man's case was curious : four of his brothers had been killed the previous year at Bamean, and he had at the same time received a bullet in the head, which, as there was but one hole was thought to have penetrated his brain; to the surprise of every one he recovered, but as the brain was injured, and only covered by a thin skin, he was thought unfit for further service, and only waited an opportunity to return to India.

as the wheel. The same process was commenced with me ; but as I was alive and conscious, my objections I presume got me a lift at the head. I well remember that when set down inside, I came to the conclusion I was not "killed," that I sat up, and that when the enemy advanced again and there was in consequence a fresh alarm, I got up, took my part in their repulse, and forgot all about the matter. When night set in, the combat was for a time closed. I went into the Barracks, and there meeting the Doctor, remembered that I was badly wounded. I learnt the sad news of the death of my beloved Commander, and yet felt relief, as I felt it would have been impossible to move him in any exigency. The fact was kept secret, that the troops might not be disheartened. When I had the Doctor apart, I told him that I feared I was badly wounded. He took me into an inner room for examination, that the disaster might not be known.

The Doctor removed my neck cloth with the utmost care, opened my shirt collar which adhered slightly to my throat, and on looking burst out laughing, telling me I was not wounded at all ! The truth is that partly owing to the fact that I had on an extremely thick silk neckerchief, consisting of a square yard of Mooltan silk, and partly owing to the obliquity with which the ball struck me, I had only received a severe blow on the front of the spine and an abrasion of the skin sufficient to let out a very little blood. There was a red mark on the skin, as though a finger smeared with blood had passed over it, and no more.

We were compelled to withdraw from the outposts in the evening. Our numbers were much diminished, and the men quite worn out with fasting and fatigue. To this was added the fact that we had now no water in the canal to protect, and therefore little object in maintaining the outposts in front of it.

At night secretly and silently a grave was dug on the east (or Nijran side) of a small building we were erecting in the Barrack Square as a magazine, and to it were committed the remains of my dear comrades Salusbury and Codrington. I do not remember when or where Sergeant Byrne was buried. My friend's grave was smoothed down, and straw burnt over it afterwards to conceal it, as I wished to keep the sad news as much as possible from the men. We passed the night much as usual, but this night and the following day there was an inexpressible feeling of relief from the fact of our having given up all our outposts, except

Khojeh Meer Khan's Fort. We had in fact not more and probably much less than half the space to defend.

The 7th was ushered in as previous days had been, and as the remaining days especially were. I will for once describe it. As soon at it was broad day the enemy, in obedience to their drums which had been beating for an hour or two before, came forth from the town and formed a perfect cordon round us. There was a broad band on all sides, just out of musket shot,* from which the enemy stole out marksmen under cover of little piles of stones, as opportunity offered. The cover we had abandoned in front too, was completely occupied; also the target butt and the oratory. It was now the Ramazan, and in the evening the enemy withdrew to break their fast, leaving heavy pickets of Cavalry and Infantry on three sides of us and in the gardens in front. In the course of the day we became aware of another loss. Shots began to drop into the interior of our square. At first these came palpably from the posts in front through the open gate way, and here I have to tell a sad tale which Mahomedans would consider especially illustrative of the doctrine of fate. Captain Codrington had a clerk, a native of Chandernagor in Bengal. This man was a Hindoo, and spoke English and French fluently. He was a very good man, but eminently timid. Regard for his old master had induced him to come to Afghanistan. When fighting began, he disappeared, nor did I hear anything of him till this time. I heard he was wounded, and went to see him. I found him crouched up in a corner of an inner room, that is a room inside another, facing the gateway. He had taken refuge here, as the most safe position he could think of. A bullet found him out, having passed through the Barrack gateway, and the two doorways of the apartments opposite, into a remote corner. Another man, a tall, stout native of the Punjab, a Hindoo I believe, named Hassa Sing, chowdree of the bazar, or—to put the term in the most intelligible English I can think of— "Clerk of the Market" of the Regiment, was also mortally wounded in the stomach, in a room a little to the north. Pottinger who was in an upper room opposite to the gateway, was good enough to lend several rifles, his private property which he had brought from Lughmanee, to our marksmen, and I think it was at his suggestion that scaffolding was erected in his room and the upper part of the wall loopholed : also cover formed by boxes to shelter one or two men placed on the roof. The more

---

* We had only " Brown Bess," with flint locks.

immediate remedy adopted was to hang a curtain behind the gateway. We then fixed the eighteen pounder there, and filled up the space at the sides with the material provided for making the gate. But this was found to be a partial remedy, bullets penetrated the rooms on the south side of our Barracks through the doorways. The women inside were much alarmed, and the men on the roofs of the houses were killed and wounded. It was quickly found out that the fire proceeded from Khojeh Meer Khan's castle which commanded the interior of our square, and that our garrison there had succumbed. The only thing we could do was to put up the walls of the officers tents on the roofs of the Barracks on the north and south sides, so as to prevent the enemy from taking aim at the men behind them. ·This dodge is known · to the Japanese, and has been practised recently by them. It proved a wonderfully efficient expedient, and although we could not prevent some of the gun bullocks and ponies being killed, the arrangement at once reduced our mortality. Who would think of canvas stopping a bullet? It could not do so, but it stopped firing! Men would not fire aimlessly.

It appears that the Soobadar commanding the Goorkhas in Khojeh Meer Khan's Fort had been talked over by the Mahomedan Moonshee,* a native of Peshawar, into surrendering. I don't blame either; the Moonshee was probably much better informed than we were of the actual state of affairs, and considered our case hopeless. The Soobadar felt doubtless that he could not hold out. The place was too large in any case for efficient defence by fifty men without water; and forming, as it did, the side of a narrow street, it was easily mined by an enemy, who had cover up to the door. The Soobadar, I believe, might have retreated to us with some loss, and in failing to do so only, I blame him ; the place was untenable. He came over to us with some proposals for surrender, the reply to which was an invitation to the Chiefs to confer. We had not heard of the cause of the outbreak, or the objects or wishes of the enemy, and hoped in any case to gain some information, all other sources being cut off.

On the 8th, two chiefs came forward to treat. They were, I believe, natives of Nijrow. I took them to Pottinger to confer with him, while I guarded against what we so much feared— treachery. I learned that Major P. had a long conversation with them, the upshot of which may be briefly summed up. They

* Sent to act as an interpreter.

believed they were acting under orders of the King to expel us.* P. said, " Produce the King's order, and we will at once evacuate the country." I know no more of this than I heard from Major Pottinger. The impression made on my mind was, that these men had been deceived, and had acted in good faith ; certain it is that after this conference, the number of our besiegers was visibly diminished. I will now enumerate all the other attempts made to treat with us : all the persons who came were referred to Major Pottinger. One came on behalf of a chief of Nijrow or Tughao, and demanded guns, money, and I don't know what, to be surrendered. After Pottinger had had his opportunity of extracting information, I told the man that I positively prohibited any one coming with such communications (which I perceived reached the men† and were most demoralizing), and I said, " If you do come, it will be at your peril. I will hang you."

Another day a chief, a genuine Afghan of bold and defiant manner, procured a cessation of firing, and forced himself in to have an interview with Pottinger. I don't know what passed. But it was plain to me he came merely for the sake of spying. I showed him round the place, told him I fully saw his object, and pointing to the bastion the Afghans had blown up, showed him how easy it was, and challenged him to come up that way if he could. He was the perfection of health and strength, but I don't think he quite approved of the spirit he found inside our place.

The last offer to treat was conveyed by the man I had promised to hang if he came again. I had then made up my mind it was impossible to hold out, and felt it would be an useless act of cruelty to put him to death. I, therefore, merely put him in ward, blindfolding him with my own pocket handkerchief, begrimed with the smoke of ten day's fighting. I regret that a Bactrian coin of Lysias, purchased a day before the outbreak, remained tied up in the corner. We felt, I believe, one and all, that it was utterly futile to treat with the enemy, and, further, when we came to know what had happened at Kabool, that it was our duty to hold out to the last, as our conquest would

* This is fully accounted for by the fact that documents forged by the rebels, but bearing the King's seal, were in circulation.

† The men crowded to hear what passed, and those who could not get within hearing, questioned those who had heard—discussion ensued which was unsuited to our position.

release the people who were besieging us, and leave them at liberty to aid those already pressing heavily on Kabool.

I think it was this afternoon we buried the dead. I most fortunately insisted on the Doctor examining every body before it was buried. One fine young man, who had laid a day or two with the dead, having been shot through the throat, was found to be quite alive and conscious. We buried forty-four in the great pit dug for a tank, but those killed at Lughmanee, on the retreat to Char-ee-kar, and at the outposts, lay unburied where they fell. Foolishly we would not bury the horses and cattle killed by the enemy's fire in the same place. They were quartered and thrown over the wall, in the hope that we would have an opportunity of removing them to a distance. This never occurred, and the stench became abominable.

We were subjected every night to the annoyance of false attacks, the real nature of which I did not know at the time. They were solely intended to wear us out. These facts I learned afterwards when a prisoner. One favourite plan was to keep drums beating for hours, and a large body of men in the bed of the canal in front, shouting, "Dum-ee-Char-yar,"* and other Afghan war cries. I afterwards learnt that these were chiefly unarmed peaceful men, residents of the town, who were compelled to turn out thus, sore against their will, while the bulk of the warriors took their rest. Eventually an occurrence took place which put an effectual stop to this.

9th. I believe it was on this day that all hope of relief was destroyed. About midday it was announced to me that a body of men were visible coming from the direction of Kabool. I at once went to look out, and saw them sure enough; but were they the relief long expected, or enemies? Relief certainly. I could make them out distinctly with a telescope. The foremost were horsemen, our own 5th Cavalry, a fact rendered certain by their white head dresses; we congratulated one another, and tears of joy streamed from my eyes; but, alas! it soon appeared we were deceived. The fantastic play of mirage had so acted on a herd of cattle grazing, as entirely to deceive us. In the evening a Syud, I believe of the family at Istalif, came in, and gave us the first news from Kabool, viz., that Burnes was killed, guns

---

* " The Life of the Four Friends ; " that is, of the four companions of Mahomet.

(Warburton's no doubt) had been captured, and that fighting occurred daily.

The enemy kept us closely besieged. It was impossible on the east side for anybody to show his head without getting a volley. In fact, it was a favourite amusement to put a Sepoy's hat (one of the old Belltoppers) on a stick and show it above the wall, and after the enemy had spent a good deal of powder and shot, to show them what they had been firing at, giving at the same time a derisive shout. Exposing myself incautiously for a few seconds, I received as I thought a ball in the elbow about the "funny bone;" my arm dropped so promptly that I did not doubt but that the bone was smashed. Taking off my coat, however, it appeared that the limb had only been struck by a spent ball, which left a painful bruise and nothing worse. Here I may remark that we found the Afghans so short of lead that many of their bullets were only quartz pebbles covered with lead. This day I shored up the flat roofs of the barracks, and cut open the gorge of the bastion next the town, and mounted a six-pounder there.* The other one was brought into play down below. There was a heavy picket of the enemy's infantry and cavalry kept by night at the back of our barracks, between us and the hills, which entirely defeated a project for getting at night a supply of water from the Khoja-seh-Yaran spring. The subadar of artillery undertook to dislodge them. He brought one of our field pieces to the side of the barrack square, furthest from that on which the picket was, and mounting the barrack roof, with the aid of a plumb line, he laid the gun in the same way that a mortar is laid, and elevating it sufficiently, fired over the opposite wall. Several shots were dropped in the middle of the picket, the men of which were just making themselves comfortable for the night. They were sent scampering, but only to take up a worse position for our interests, viz., nearer to the coveted source of water.

In the evening some Afghans crept into the huts fronting the south-east corner of our barracks, and commenced singing vociferously. This was thought to be a piece of bravado. Some thought they were mining; I knew well they could not reach us before day, and that they would not venture to continue there during daylight, and that I could completely destroy their work

* It had been kept below for possible service outside; the second one was not to be depended upon.

at dawn if they were mining ; so contented myself with visiting
the sentries perpetually, telling them to keep a good look out.
In each of the bastions a subadar was stationed, excepting the
north-west one held by Mr. Rose. I kept my usual post seated
in a chair at the gateway, where I had a small reserve ready to
act in any direction as requisite ; the remainder of the regiment
who survived unwounded were perpetually on duty on what I
may call the walls—as many as could lay in each bastion ; the
others on the flat roofs, above which the walls rose from eighteen
inches to three feet. The lowest parts were slightly protected by
stones and billets of wood placed upon the top. After midnight
there was a sudden explosion, alarm, and a general firing by the
enemy. It appears they had excavated into the south-east bastion and blown up the front of it. There was no mining from the
huts, but a man had boldly sat at the foot of the bastion and dug
a hole into it, which he loaded with powder, tamped and fired.
The singing was intended to distract attention from his operations. The digging was distinctly heard by the women in the
barrack below, but the subadar neglected the information conveyed to him. The men instantly deserted that quarter, and it
was believed the enemy were among us, but I got together the
reserve, and in a minute or two was in the breach. I found that
it was unoccupied, and quickly barricaded it, so as to render it
as strong as before The enemy had made no attempt to take
advantage of what had been done. Had they advanced with a
storming party, the place would have been theirs in all probability, instead of which they merely indulged in a desultory fire.
After this a piece of lighted port-fire was dropped over the walls
at each bastion every half hour, so as to enable us to see what
was going on below.

10th. Since the supply of water failed from the canal and we
had been confined to the barracks, the practice was to open the
Postern Gate, a small, narrow one, for a short time after dark,
and allow the garrison to go out to get their supply from the pit,
where it had been received for building purposes before the
siege, and from the hollows round the walls where earth was
obtained for their construction. This measure I had to superin-
tend myself, as from the narrowness of the entry and the eager-
ness of the people, there was great danger of a crush, and much
of the water was spilt. This evening the last drops of water

remaining were collected in pitchers, and brought in and placed under sentries in a room.

11th. Water was served out to fighting men only. At first, referring to the fact that the corps was composed entirely of Hindoos, I ordered a native officer to serve it out; but quickly a cry of partiality was raised, and the men insisted that I should serve it out. I did serve out water on this and the succeeding day as far as it would go, about half a tea cup* full to each man. Those who know Hindoo prejudices on the subject, and remember that every man, from the Brahmin and Rajpoot downward, lost his caste by thus receiving water in a tea cup from my hand, will be able to realize in a measure the amount of suffering which the men had undergone to induce them to make such a sacrifice. Yet all appeared staunch, I heard no murmuring One of our Mahomedan gunners had deserted it is true. The rest, to be sure, had asked for their pay on the pretext that they had not the means of buying food at the regimental shops; but I had a plain answer : I had not received it; and, to obviate difficulty, ordered credit should be given them. I allowed them and the Sepoys generally as much mutton as they could eat from the officers' mess flock; little was used, as they said it only made them more thirsty. I learnt afterwards that many sucked the raw flesh to assuage their thirst. Fighting is at all times dry work, but fighting without water is nearly impossible. The misery was great; the Hindoos, accustomed to daily ablutions, had not bathed since the commencement of the affair. Even at the time that we were still unconfined to our barracks, food was only obtainable at irregular intervals; our voices were hoarse, our lips cracked, our faces begrimed with dust and smoke, and our eyes blood-shot. I do not remember to have sat down to a meal after the evening on which Pottinger joined us, my food being chiefly dried mulberries obtained from the Fakeer's Tukeea in front, or fried flour brought to me by the Sepoys. Truly we were one. There was, however, an article of diet without which I don't think I could have held out. Each morning before daylight Captain Codrington's servant brought me a cup of tea. The last was, I think, on the morning of the 12th, and was from a small vessel of water which Mr. Rose had secured. This was the sole source of supply for himself, Major Pottinger, the Doctor,

*Much of this was mere mud.

and myself, and certainly for two days, if not three, beyond the small cup of tea I tasted no fluid.

In the evening I sent out a party[*] by stealth to endeavour to get a supply of water by passing between the enemy's pickets, and getting in rear of the town, to the spot where the water from the canal which had been cut ran down. They got a little water, but alarmed the enemy, and lost the greater part of what they were bringing in; what came was at once seized and drank by whoever could get hold of it. One or two of the party were reported to have been captured by the enemy.

12th. We were in every way, as might be supposed, much worse off. Since rain fell on the night of the 5th, the weather, especially at night, had become much colder, the mountain tops being covered with snow. Our men were almost entirely worn out, the enemy used all sorts of contrivances to dispirit us. Scaling ladders were for several days paraded round us, though in several places the enemy could get in without using them, as they could reach the top of the wall from the outside with their hands. There was usually one general attack per diem, and it did not fail to-day; many men were absent from their posts, and I had to drive them up from their barracks. During the fight some slunk away again, and among these a native officer. I discovered him in the corner of a room, behind a screen, with fire in a chafing dish burning before him, mumbling "Muntras" or magic formulæ. It was needful to make an example, so I pulled him out by the collar, tore his coat off, and set him to work as a coolie with the camp followers. We were attempting to fill up the unfinished magazine with earth, intending to convert it into a Cavalier, on which to mount our second gun, so as to command the breach made by the enemy in our south-east bastion. I was soon obliged to give it up, and admit the validity of the excuse made by the poor people, who said they could not work without water.

I organized an expedition to attempt again to get water this evening, and intended myself to command it; but the native officers of the corps conjured me not to go out, as they said, if

[*] This expedition was prompted by the fact that some had let themselves down over the walls, whence they had stolen to the back of the town and obtained water. The measure was so bold that, but for the success of these adventures, I should not have thought of it.

anything happened to me, they had no* one to look to for guidance. I felt compelled to give in, and yet, feeling the absolute necessity of keeping the men in strict control, I placed the expedition under the orders of Mr. Rose and our best native officer. I indicated the points they were to hold till the water carriers returned, and did all in my power to ensure success. The urgent necessity for absolute silence was pointed out to all, and I had good hope that we might succeed in getting enough water to last for a day or two. After a long and anxious interval we were amazed by firing close to us—a volley at the building intended for a mess house and another at the canal, followed by scattered firing in the same direction, and then from the enemy's pickets. By-and-bye the detachment returned, rampant with triumph, but without water, or scarcely any. Whatever quantity came was at once consumed or disposed of privately. Rose brought two standards captured from the enemy. The first thing I learnt was, that my plan had entirely failed. The posts indicated by me were not taken up, which, considering that all were suffering the agonies of thirst, was not to be wondered at. All rushed to the water, which was reached without detection, they then drank their fill, and instead of following up the plan laid down, which might still have been adopted in part, conceived the idea of falling on the pickets of the enemy in front of our position. This view was carried out, and I believe the picket at the mess house and at the canal were attacked at the same time. It was found that the whole of them had gone to sleep, without planting a sentry; they were in fact enjoying their first sleep after a day's hard work and a heavy meal, for it was now the Ramzan, during which they fasted all day till the sun went down. Poor people! to the majority it was also their last sleep. I was told that the mess house being surrounded and aim being taken, the first volley was fired, and those not killed by it were bayonetted.

Almost simultaneously a similar event took place at the canal, the party near which were chiefly mere "claqueurs," driven there to annoy us by yells : some of these escaped. However, the enemy received a terrible blow, but the success appeared to me quite useless. The object for which the party was sent forth had entirely failed, and we were dying of thirst. I had a horror of the destruction of even such men as the Afghans were by such

---

* The only remaining officer of the regiment, Mr. Rose, was very young; he had joined the service but a few months previously.

means. It seemed unmanly. To be sure they would only have been too glad to treat us in the same way, if they* could. Our black† bearded visitor who was a Chief of some distinction, was among the dead; great lamentation was made over him next day.

13*th*. The failure of our attempts to obtain water, except for the few who went forth, made it manifest we could no longer hold out. All the hope we ever had of relief from Kabool had long since vanished; and it was clear we must either die where we were or effect some change in our circumstances. As our position was palpably untenable, the probability of having to effect a retreat had been often in our minds from the first; but it was combined with the hope of assistance from Kabool; for no one needed to be told that a retreat over from forty to fifty miles of country in open rebellion was impossible to people so out-numbered that they could not show their noses outside their Barracks. We had no means of carrying our wounded, and so early as the date of the death of the gallant Codrington I felt inexpressible relief from that event, as I was well aware that in the event of it being necessary to remove him, he could not bear the motion of the single doolee or litter we had for carrying the wounded. There were a great number of considerations which negatived even an attempt at retreat till this day. In the forenoon, however, the native Officers in a body came towards me. I had noticed whisperings and consultations in twos and threes among them, and did not require any one to tell me what it meant. As they drew near, I understood their errand only too well. They respectfully announced that "something must be done," as it was impossible they could hold out any longer without water. I had quite made up my mind too on the subject, and in reply pledged my life on the attempt to lead them to water that night. Now for the first time a council was held in the room where Pottinger lay wounded, at which the Doctor and Mr. Rose, I believe, assisted. The question of retreat or no retreat was not discussed. The only alternative to my mind was to attempt to seize by surprise some native castle in which we might expect to find some food and have access to water, but I could not call to mind a single one from which the supply could not be cut off. All were agreed that our only chance, hopeless as it seemed, lay in attempting

---

* I remember in the spring an English soldier was shot at night, as he lay asleep in his tent amidst his comrades at the Camp at Seeah Sung near Kabool. This was done in the mere wantonness of hate.

† Shah Mahmood.

to reach Kabool. If we got a good way, it was thought possible, relief might meet us and help us in. The route was the only question of debate. The direct route was the most difficult and one upon which opposition was most certain; for we had to pass several fortified villages, if we went by it. My own acquaintance with the country was imperfect, but I was disposed to take a line to the lett or S. E. which, it seemed to me, would bring us into broken ground, where the enemy's horse could not act against us, and from whence we might possibly effect a junction with Colonel Sale's Brigade, supposed to be in that direction. Pottinger and the Doctor, who both had seen much more of the country than I had, were in favour of adopting a line of road skirting the mountains, as it would give, in the event of our being cut up, the best chance of escape to the women and children and camp followers, who might perhaps be able to clamber the sides of the hills and find shelter among the rocks. There was another recommendation to this route; it would probably be unwatched, and it abounded in water; we knew too that there were some well disposed to us in the direction of Istalif. I fully concurred in these arguments, and it was understood that we would adopt the hill foot route. Our plans it was thought prudent to conceal as far as possible. Spikes were ordered to be made for the guns, but the armorer who made them, protested that they would not break, as he had no liquid in which to cool them. I suggested the use of ghee, not knowing at that time the effect of oil on steel. The Doctor urged me to save my Bactrian coins. I had a valuable collection, which I could have conveniently carried in my pockets, but as I had adopted it as a principle that all baggage was to be abandoned, I could not in my own person set the example to the contrary.

After what has been already recorded, I do not think there are many persons who would want explanation of the state which rendered retreat necessary; but I will nevertheless briefly reca·pitulate our condition. On the 2nd November we had about seven hundred and forty men, more than half of whom were recruits, and who had never been under fire. We had since then lost our Commandant, Quarter Master, Serjeant Major and, I believe, fully 100 privates killed; we had our Quarter Master Serjeant and eight barrack rooms full of wounded, probably not less than two hundred, we had lost fifty by capture. This is the lowest estimate, so that there could not remain more than three hundred and ninety worn out men under arms. We had over one hundred women and forty children, with perhaps one hundred camp followers of sorts. The whole of this party was totally destitute of water. At the commencement we had only by estimate seven days' provisions, but our store was by no means exhausted.* It probably would have carried us a week further. Our ammunition had been at starting 200 rounds per man, but had been husbanded with the greatest care ; no such random firing was allowed as I have repeatedly seen since, and our store was therefore still respectable ; we had but little ammunition for the guns, one of which had broken down thrice ; and our muskets were so foul, that it was with difficulty balls could be forced into them; even urine could not be obtained to wash them out. We were closely besieged by overwhelming numbers, and could not show ourselves outside in daylight; all hope of relief had vanished ; and to us remained alone the choice of death, surrender to a notoriously faithless enemy, or the attempt to join by stealth our comrades at Kabool. I had received from two men, the armorer and the native doctor, one a native of the Punjab and the other of Cashmere, hints that treachery was brewing among the gunners; but I could get no tangible explanation from them of the grounds for their supposition. The gunners had behaved as well as men could do. They fought bravely, and had lost twelve men out of fifty-six, their entire number. As I then said, they were as my right arm to me ; I could not therefore either punish them on vague suspicion, nor could I even turn them out of the barracks, possibly to increase the enemy's ranks, especially as their accusers had shewn no courage themselves. Indeed the native doctor was reputed an arrant coward. I did what I deemed right, and gave private instructions that a vigilant eye should be kept on them.

The precise nature of our expedition to take place in the evening was for good reasons kept secret; but I had openly pledged my word to do something, and the necessity for making spikes for the guns, in anticipation of having to abandon them, would have betrayed our objects, if all were so dull as not to be able to form a pretty good guess. We never had draught carriage for all three guns, and as the bullocks had been entirely without water from the 6th, if not before, and altogether without food for five days, as indeed all our beasts were, it was hopeless to expect them to do service. The armorer had just shown me

* Chiefly from want of water to cook with.

the spikes, and explained his difficulty about rendering them
brittle, and a cessation of firing occurring at this time, I went up
to the N. E. Bastion to see "what was up." Ensign Rose was
with me, and also the Subadar of artillery. I saw a native of
India, with clean clothes and combed hair, coming towards the
gateway. I asked, observing he was an artilleryman, whether
he was the man who had deserted, or whether he was the man
cut off in the attempt to obtain a supply of water. The Subadar
at once gave answer that he was the deserter. In any case it
was plain that the enemy had sent him, probably to offer terms;
and as I was quite determined not to make any, being completely
assured that none made with us would be kept, I felt it of importance to prevent his holding any communication with the men
At this time I was unarmed. I met the man as he came in, and
seized him by the collar with my left hand as he attempted to
pass me. Instantly he threw himself on the ground, I still holding him; this reduced me to a stooping posture, in which I
received a tremendous blow on the neck, which I conjecture was
followed by one or two more. I started, letting go my man, and
turning round, at the same time feeling a sharp pain in my right
wrist; I saw the blood spouting in a long jet from it, and the
Subadar glaring at me like a demon, holding a sword with both
hands, and in the act of striking at me again. All this was the
work of an instant. I had the whole of the muscles* on one side
of the back of my neck severed, a severe cut into the right
shoulder joint, another in the right wrist, nearly severing my
hand, and a fourth in the left fore arm, splintering the bone. I
retreated up a ladder to the roof of the barracks, and shouted
"Treachery," calling on the men to fire on the gunners, who
were escaping *en masse*. I, however, after having the limb
with its spouting artery bound, found myself so faint from loss of
blood that I could not stand. I was conducted between two men
into the lower storey of the building, in which was Pottinger,
and was laid on a bed. The enemy made a most vigorous attack
on all sides. Pottinger had himself carried to the gate, where
the Doctor, with one or two men, vigorously worked the eighteen-
pounder, and by dark the enemy had been completely repulsed.
I heard afterwards that the artillerymen, seeing our affairs were
desperate, thought it best to make terms for themselves. The

---

* A bad tailor, who had made one of the most prodigious collars ever seen, was
probably the unintentional means of saving my life.

arrangement was, they were to kill me as a proof of their zeal, and to go over to the enemy, who were to make a general attack in the confusion which would ensue, and take the place by escalade. It was expected no one would remain to work the guns; on this point, and in the anticipated success, calculations failed. It appears that from some sign the Subadar understood all was settled. He, therefore, when I left his side, snatched a sword from the hands of Ensign Rose, and followed me. I presume, when the man I had seized, whose face was toward the Subadar, saw him coming at me, he threw himself down to be out of the way of the blow.

Major Pottinger, the Doctor, and Mr. Rose, after driving off the enemy, attempted to organize a retreat, but this was out of the question; none of them but Rose belonged to the corps, and he was too young and unused to command. The men, women, and camp followers began to load themselves with whatever they could find. A Goorkha Jemadar served the cash* in the regimental chest out to whoever would take it. The Doctor spiked the guns, and it was proposed to blow up the magazine, but 1 negatived this, for two reasons. It would be sure to arouse the attention of the enemy, and thereby defeat our attempt to escape secretly; and probably it would destroy our wounded, who were unable to move. I have said, discipline was at an end, but still there was some attempt made at order. It was arranged that after dark the force should be divided : one half to leave by the main entrance, and the other half by the postern gate; both parties were to unite on the parade ground, and proceed in silence by the route previously determined. When all was nearly ready the Doctor came to me. An assistant made a light with a piece of oiled rag, and the Doctor amputated my right hand at the wrist joint, rapidly sewing the skin together with three stitches of a needle and thread. As may be supposed, I was dreadfully faint, but not a drop of liquid of any kind was to be found, some ether excepted. Tinctures of all sorts had disappeared from the Hospital, the smell of the ether luckily had been too powerful, and a drink of it revived me. I was put on horseback and led out by the postern, a man holding me on either side, to the parade ground. There we waited unavailingly for the other party;

* The man's name was Hunooman Singa Jemadar. He had been from Nepal to Pekin with tribute. He measured out the money with a brass lotah or drinking vessel. He was a brave soldier.

a man was sent back to bring them on ; he did not, I believe, return. While waiting, an infant began to cry ; the Doctor said he would silence it, and he did so for ever, I was told, by dashing it on the ground.* He went back himself in search after the missing men but did not return to us. At last we started, Pottinger leading. I continued to be held by a man either side of my horse, with a cushion under my chin to keep my head up. After travelling about four miles, we came to water. It was difficult to get the party to move at all from this, and I was told that many never did so.

Pottinger was fully impressed with the fact that in speed and secrecy alone had we a chance of escape ; he therefore urged the party on. Rose and the Quarter Master Sergeant Hanrahan (who had recoved from the wound received on 4th November) were to bring up the rear, but this was found impossible. We waited and halted repeatedly, with the result of constantly diminishing numbers. At I think about 1 A. M. we heard firing to the left at Kalabagh on the main road, which I afterwards ascertained arose from the detection of the party which had failed to join us on leaving the barrack. I think it was some time before we got to Istalif, that we missed Ensign Rose, Serjeant Hanrahan and the men with them. Pottinger's object was to draw them on as fast as he could, and to show the way, waiting occasionally in difficult places for them to come up. We had travelled about twenty miles, when we missed them, and all endeavours failed to discover them again.† It was clear that they had taken some other path, so having no choice, we pushed on, our party diminihed to seven or eight. We stumbled on a water mill, with the miller awake and busy, he too readily came out with a welcome which we dared not return, but on the contrary avoided. We struggled on, continually losing our way in the dark till day began to dawn, when we found ourselves under the walls of a fortified village, beyond which was a naked hill. The majority of our party were in favour of taking to this hill, for the sake of concealment. I felt very strongly, however, that when our evacuation of Charee-kar was known, the enemy would be sure to look for us in such

---

* This was confirmed by an eye-witness in 1871.

† Pottinger feelings and mine probably differed. He had been nine days in bed and was consequently cool. I had been the whole of the time in constant excitement. He did not belong to the Regiment. I did. Nothing would have induced me to part company with my men as long as they would follow me. He now looked upon them as what they really were, a disorderly mob, useless as soldiers. This is written with reference to remarks in his narrative.

a situation. I recommended we should take shelter in some ravines channeling the otherwise almost level plain near the village, where I felt assured the enemy would never dream of looking for us. It was indeed fortunate that we did so, for what I anticipated occurred; the enemy were seen hunting, and firing at some of our men on the hill side, while we lay at hand closely concealed. Once indeed a party came up to within two hundred yards of us, but turned back without seeing us. Our party now consisted of Major Pottinger, myself, the Major's Goorkha* Moushee named Mohun Beer, all mounted, my orderly Maun Sing, and a Regimental sutler on foot. I must not, however, forget Major Pottinger's bull terrier, of whose barking I was apprehensive when the enemy approached us, but who was, I was assured, too tired to bark. During the night I had drunk water liberally, and I believe about half a pint of ether. During this terrible day the largest share of the little water with our party, was given to me. I had also some dried mulberries to eat. As soon as it was well dark, we pushed on again, Pottinger guiding; we passed close to Killa Ultifat, a castle where the dogs alone took notice of us, and crossed an open plain to the last range of hills dividing us from Kabool. Now I knew of only two roads crossing it, both of which were sure to be watched; but Pottinger, who had frequently passed and repassed, knew of a goat path between them, but he had never trodden it, and in any case it would be a tough job for a horse to cross the hill by it. We pushed on for this path, but failing to find it, attempted the hill side. Weak as I was from loss of blood, I could not keep my seat, and several times slipped off; on the last occasion I was very badly bruised by the stones on which I fell. It appeared to me hopeless to think of getting further. I therefore entreated Pottinger to leave me to my fate, and attend to his own safety. He most nobly and generously refused to do so. He told me to lie quiet and rest myself, while he made search for a path. This he found, and then rested for a while himself. After about an hour's delay, I was remounted, and we succeeded in crossing the mountain, but at the foot of it to our horror found ourselves in an encampment of nomad Afghan shepherds, whose black goat's hair tents we could not see till we were among them. Their dogs barked furiously, but luckily the night was bitterly cold, and no one had the courage to face it. There were two ways from this camp, we chose one to the right; we hoped by skirting the lake which here lay between us and Kabool, to get into the cantonments at the side furthest from the town, but Pottinger could not find the way, so we were compelled to push on for Deh-Afghana, a large castle in the suburbs of the town of Kabool, under the walls of which we needs must pass. There were sentries on the towers who challenged us. Pottinger answered in Persian, strongly flavoured with a Milesian accent, that we were the servants of a native chief whom he named. The answer was not quite satisfactory, for the sentry said, "Stop, I'll come down." Our side replied, "All right," and calculating when our friend had commenced his descent, we pushed on as fast as we could get our horses to go. We got into the town, and in the outskirts dropped our sutler, at the semi-fortified house of one of the Hindoo Shikarporee merchants. He, poor man, to be sure, had had no fighting, but he had been several days without water. He had with him a large bundle of property, which he conveyed into his stronghold. Maun Sing, my orderly, who was also on foot, declined the option of remaining here, and determined to share the remaining danger with us. We thought of making for the Bala Hissar, where we hoped to be received by the king, but for some reason changed our plan. We passed nearly through the city, meeting only one single person awake, a fakeer, smoking his pipe, who gave us his blessing as we passed. We got into the path leading to the cantonment, and were near the end of it, when, to our horror, we found the open shops on either side of the way, which was not twenty feet wide, filled with men. We were called upon to stop, but did not. Then arose a cry of "Stop them," "Infidels," etc., etc., followed up by a fusillade which did no injury to any one but perhaps themselves. Truly in this, as in so many other instances, Providence protected us, for if any had had the courage to put out his hand and seize our bridles, we had been lost. The fire put a little spirit into our weary animals, who took us clear of them. Maun Sing kept up with us. And here I must correct a mistake into which Pottinger has fallen in his account. He says Maun Sing's accoutrements were hid by a Posteen or sheep's-skin cloak; this is a mistake, of which I was further assured by Maun Sing himself five or six years afterwards. A man could not possibly have made such a march, still less run for his life, clothed in such a garment. I believe it was Maun Sing's cross belts and breast plate that first disclosed who we were. Our troubles were not yet at an end. The firing had roused the English garrison, and we were challenged by sentries in a large fort to our right, then in succession by those to our left in the cantonment field work, and we had no small difficulty in passing the jealous and inexorable sentries round two and a half sides of it to the only gate by which we could get access. Here I was taken off my horse, and for the first time had my wounds dressed in the guard-room. *Then* I felt that if it had been to save me from immediate death, I could not have gone ten yards further. We were, to use the words of Eyre, received "as men who had risen from the dead."

Though this is intended to be a personal narrative, I cannot refrain from giving some account of the fate of my comrades. I enjoyed peculiar opportunities of learning particulars from the Afghans themselves during the many months spent in captivity among them; and also from having collected the survivors of the corps in 1842, and conducted them back to India.

It appears then that the Doctor, when he went back to the Barrack from the parade ground, found that the party which should have joined us, had taken the direct road to Kabool; he joined them and, I presume, failed to induce the men to return. The party was fired upon while passing through the fortified village of Kala Bagh at about 1 A. M., and this we heard. They struggled on till daylight, when they had a fight with the enemy crossing a hill I believe at Ak-Serac, where the man who gave me these particulars was badly wounded with a spear and taken prisoner. All the rest of this party, excepting the Doctor, were here either killed, or wounded and taken prisoners. The Doctor, who was mounted, managed to get clear, and by nine or ten o'clock had got nearly to the foot of the last range between Char-ee-kar and Kabool; the range which we crossed next night. Had he succeeded in ascending it, he would have found the pass occupied, but he was not fated to do so. He met some labourers from the town. They surrounded him. He gave one his horse, another his sword,* a third his pistols, and in fact divested himself of all he had, walking on afoot. His

* This sword had belonged to Lieutenant Rattray, killed at Char-ee-kar, regarding which there is a story told by Pottinger, which I saw in one of the English papers in 1843. Rattray bought this sword from the widow of its last owner, who met a violent death. The tradition was that every owner, from the time of Nadir Shah in 1740, had met with a violent death. It was offered to me, being a fine Damascus blade, but I declined to have an article with such an ominous legend attached to it. The Doctor in consequence kept it for himself.

horse no doubt had given in. One of the wood-cutters followed him, and, to use his own words as communicated to me, felled him with his axe " for the love of God. "

Ensign Rose and Serjeant Hanrahan, with those men who adhered to them, as has already been narrated, followed the same track as ourselves, or nearly so, as far as Istalif; they kept to the foot of the western hills, and by morning had gained the Mama Khatoon pass in advance of us, to our right, when they were surrounded and cut up. All accounts I have received, agree in stating that they made a gallant defence* and fought hard for their lives. I think up to the time of the retreat of the army from Kabool, only one, or at the outside two, of the corps had found their way into cantonment; but one man, Motee Ram Havildar, actually found his way past Jellalabad to India.†

After General Pollock's advance, I collected 165 men, survivors of the Regiment, who were distributed to the Goorkha Regiments in India. Maun Sing was honoured and promoted : a love affair, however, got him into difficulty, and he, knowing his countrymen well, fled for his life; but he was befriended by Captain (now General) Troup, whom he had attended as an orderly during the retreat from Kabool. He was enlisted in the 48th N. I., and was engaged in the battles of the first Seik war where he lost his thumb, while orderly to Major George Broadfoot, then Governor-General Agent, who lost his life on that occasion. Maun Sing was pensioned, and had beside the Order of Merit to which a pension was attached. He came all the way from Almorah to Chyabassa, in August 1848, to see me, since when I have not heard of him

Most of the wounded who were unable to move out from Char-ee-kar with us, were slaughtered next day. It is curious that the enemy either did not discover our retreat, or were afraid to venture near, till long after daylight. We had all throughout the siege sounded our bugles with the regularity of peaceable times, by way of a hint to the enemy that we were all right. On this last fatal morning, the Bugle Major, of whose gallantry I have already spoken, and who was too severely wounded to leave with us, crawled up to a Bastion and sounded the customary bugle at dawn.

* Forty or fifty were taken prisoners, amongst whom were Oomer Sing, the senior Subadar, and his wife. The Subadar of Artillery who wounded me, passing the castle where this man was a prisoner, caused him to be put to death, and the poor Subadar's widow, long a prisoner, used to go daily to weep over his bleaching bones.

† One of the survivors, I met at Buxa, Bootan (!), January, 1867.

F CHAF

BY MOTEERA

IITON'S RECOLL
++ *Tombs*
of European offic

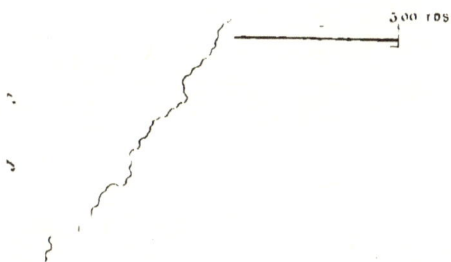

500 105

 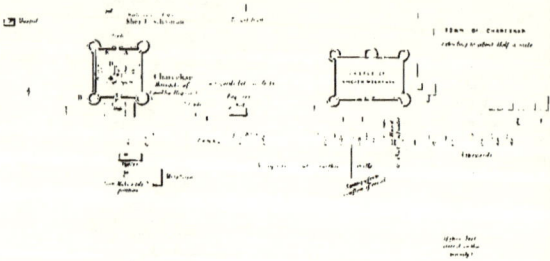

APPENDIX A.

Copy of Letter from Major Eldred Pottinger to
R. Haughton, Esq.

Village of Bynoh Hissar, one and a half miles east of Kabool,
29th May, 1842.

My dear Mr. Haughton,

I was gratified by your letter of the 26th of February,
only a few days received, or should have answered it earlier, for
I can assure you, I can most fully sympathize with your anxiety
about your gallant son Your prediction of non-relief from
anxiety has long ere this proved true, showing how correctly
you viewed our situation.

Your son was cut down in a mutiny of the artillerymen, previous to our evacuation of the fortified barrack of Char-ee-kar,
and no language I am master of is sufficient to express my
admiration of the fortitude and resolution he showed. It was
particularly owing to his example and his exertions, that we
were able to hold out as long as we did ; and before Captain Codrington, his commanding Officer, died, he requested me to make
special mention of him to the Government, and to represent to Sir
William Macnaghten, that his conduct had shewn him well fitted
to command the regiment The wounds he received, there was
not time to dress before we marched, so that he had to bear up
against their pain for two nights and a day.

When we left Kabool, he was left behind : the two sword cuts
on his shoulder and neck were nearly well, as was that on his
left arm, while the stump of the right arm was rapidly improving.

Since my being brought here, I have been unable to see him,
but learn by means of the servants that he is quite well again, and
I have every hope of seeing him shortly. The first opportunity
I have, I shall send him your letter; he expressed much anxiety
to send information to you, particularly on Mrs. Haughton's account, and I believe his letters were lost during our unfortunate
attempt to retreat. Haughton and I were inmates of the same
room from the time we reached camp till Sir William Macnagh-

ten's murder, when I was obliged to leave off care of self. At that period, things were as bad as they could be ; the military would neither fight nor fly, and we had neither food nor fuel. I was compelled to renew Sir William Macnaghten's convention by the same causes that he was compelled to open it, and the result, you will ere this have learned, was the utter destruction of the force. I have been preserved by giving myself up as a hostage to ensure the performance of the treaty demands ; both parties broke their pledges, and I am of course a prisoner. The ladies of the party were promised protection by Mahomed Ukbar Khan, and as our army would not protect them, and that Chief's family were in our hands, I recommended that they should take advantage of his offer, and fortunately they did, for they have been and are well treated, after the manner of the Afghans. General Pollock's force has been at Jelallabad for nearly two months, but he is paralyzed by the arrangements of Sir Jasper Nichols, of the Commissariat department, and want of definite instructions. In return for your prediction, I will also venture my opinion that, if more energy and wisdom are not shown, we shall in all probability receive another check. With General Pollock's army some of the worst officers have been sent.

The most miserable arrangements have been made, particularly in the Commissariat, so that I doubt if Pollock's ability will be able to master it, unless he has the fullest powers and support The service is excessively unpopular with both officers and men ; the former are great pecuniary losers, and the latter have been so alienated from their officers by Lord W. Bentinck's arrangements, that they have no longer that care for the service ; we no longer get the sons of respectable landholders, but the poor and needy, to keep whom in order, the lash is absolutely necessary, but not to be used, from his wise measure to gain " *Home popularity.*" Latterly every effort has been made to reduce the power of the commanding officers, and Government has, as you may see here, nearly succeeded. All our old soldiers regret the past times, however, and would rather have the old system than the new.

If the Government does not take some decided steps to recover the affections of the army, I really think a single spark will blow the Sepoys into mutiny ; for the zeal of the officers is cold, and it has been that alone which prevents the spirit hitherto. The sole cause of our defeat was not this, to be sure, but it in a great measure aided the incompetence of leaders; but every one in the force knew with what contempt military suggestions had been received, and that, joined to other causes, rendered them careless of consequences, and I believe many thought the sooner they could get back the better, and hence did not oppose our retreat. Shah Shooja was murdered at the end of February; his son, however, still holds out in the Bala Hissar or citadel, and will be able to do so, I believe, some weeks longer. If Pollock can advance before the Bala Hissar falls, he will not meet much opposition, otherwise I fear he will. Trusting you will excuse this rough scrawl, which is written sitting on the floor, with my knee as a support,

I remain, my dear Sir,

Yours very sincerely,

ELDRED POTTINGER.

APPENDIX B.

EXTRACT OF A LETTER FROM MAJOR CODRINGTON TO A FRIEND IN ENGLAND.

I wrote to you from Kabool on 28th September, when I was disappointed in my hope of being able to visit the scene of dear Christopher's gallant struggle at Char-ee-kar, but a day or two afterwards a party of horse with Sir R. Shakespere was sent to Char-ee-kar, and I got leave to join him. Henry Lawrence also accompanied us. We started, disguised as Afghans, soon after dusk, and after a fatiguing ride of forty miles reached Char-ee-kar, just as the troops had quitted the ground.

I could only therefore take a hasty glance at the place which poor Christopher defended, and where he found his grave. It does not deserve the name of Fort, it is merely a range of Sepoy' huts forming a square enclosure, the outer wall not being high enough above the roof to form a parapet. There was a broad gateway, but no gate; and opposite the small house which the officers occupied; you may conceive the difficulty of defending such a place even under favorable circumstances; but besides the defects I have mentioned, it was commanded on one side by a more lofty fort from which the party which first occupied it were drawn, the other side by rising ground. A sort of parapet was made by tearing up the tents and making sand bags : but the soil being full of pebbles, in fact composed almost entirely of them, they were scattered about when struck by a ball, and did more harm than good; not a drop of water was to be had, except when the garrison sallied forth and fought for it; and how the place was held for a fortnight against overpowering numbers, is scarcely conceivable. The bravery of the garrison must have been beyond all praise, and their exertions unremitting. In the centre of the enclosure stood the magazine, in which dear Christopher and Lieutenant Salusbury were buried in one grave; it was a mass of ruins, the walls and roof destroyed, and the exact spot undistinguishable among the mass of rubbish. I could only stay for a minute, but it was a melancholy satisfaction to stand on the spot which had been hallowed by the presence of one so dear to me, and to pay the tribute of affection over his grave. I was obliged to hurry off, to overtake the rear guard of the troops, and after a ride of ten miles further reached the new ground, thoroughly knocked up."

APPENDIX C.

Statement of PUDDUM SING, *first of Shah Shooja's 4th or Ghoorka Regiment, 8th Company, then of the 8th Company Nusseree Battalion, and now Harildar in the 8th Company 1st Goorkha Regiment—a native of Palee Pachowny Chowkole Pulli, west of Almorah. Made at Buxa, Bhoolan, January 12th,* 1867.

I was left wounded and unable to move on the evacuation of Char-ee-kar; we remained all night, expecting to be murdered. Next morning the Affghans came and stripped us of our clothing Some were killed. Heera Sing was Subadar of my Company, he was wounded in a night attack at 8 P. M. It was 8 P. M. when the troops evacuated Char-ee-kar. I remained at Char-ee-kar with the Subadar till he went into Cabul, (that is the Subadar who surrendered his post); he was a Kankee, his name was—— Adhikaree. I lay for nine months wounded at Char-ee-kar. A bunniah took me to Kalabagh, whence we fled on the advance of the troops. I met Lieutenant McKean of the Khelat-i-Ghilzee

Regiment between Ghuznee and Kandahar. He, on hearing that I was of the 4th Regiment, questioned me and put me through my facings; being satisfied, he took me to Captain Craigie, by whose orders I was enlisted in the regiment.

When we got to Cabul, I wished to join the survivors of my own corps, but was told that all regiments were the same, and that I must remain where I was. When we were encamped near Seeah Sung, I went and made my salam to you.

I was with the party who first went to the relief of Major Pottinger's Fort at Lugmanee. The 7th and 8th companies went, and the same companies were sent there again the next day, and also were engaged in the first fight at Char-ee-kar. I do not distincly remember the commencement of the outbreak, but so much that one day it was reported Mr. Rattray was killed, then the two companies were sent out. We had two men wounded, the enemy had seven or eight killed, I bayoneted one myself. I do not know the actual loss on one side or the other. That same night Mohun Beer Moonshee, Major Pottinger and a Kerance Sahib came to our place, it may have been the next night; the morning after they came, I heard from an old sepoy of my Company that the enemy had got into their Fort. So our men escaped by a postern gate. I do remember that some of our men remained on sentry at the towers at Lugmanee after the rest came away.

I was in the fight which took place at the corner of the Char-ee-kar bazar. We drove the enemy out of their first shelter, and we took cover in the canal, from which the enemy had suffered the water to escape; from thence our sepoys began to advance one or two at a time; you called out to them not to advance, as the enemy were too many for us. I remember you wrote on a piece of paper with charcoal to Captain Codrington for more men and for what else I don't know. We went on after that.

I was with Captain Codrington when he was wounded in our bazar, the people of which had gone inside the Barrack; he was wounded in the breast; I do not remember when Major Pottinger was wounded. I was wounded the night when Ensign Rose went out with two or three companies. Heramunee Soobadar and three or four of our men were killed. We passed out by the Parade ground and through the enemy's entrenchments, when Ensign Rose fired. I was then wounded in the right thigh and left arm, and became unconscious. I remained in Hospital for eight or nine days previous to the retreat.

I heard you were wounded by a Golundaz. I was lying in great pain with the wound in my leg at the time, but struggled to the door, and saw you returning towards the Hospital. People said to the sepoys who were with you, "Why did you not prevent this?" A Havildar said, "Who should know that we had an enemy within? we were watching the enemy without."

I remained with Jye Deb Brahmin, and an Eastern man whose name I don't know, for nine months, at the ash pit of Hummam (Turkish bath), for the sake of its warmth. Jye Deb was in the Battalion at Kangra, and died there.

I think there were about one hundred men left wounded or dying in Hospital. Some were killed, some were carried away. some went with Soubadar ———— Adhikari; the man lying next to me was killed, because he did not get up quick enough. I received a thrust of a bayonet. A sepoy came to the Hospital and said, the Soubadar called us. I went towards the town, but never saw him. An Akhoon fed me; after my wound healed, the limb remained stiff; he told me to rub it daily with ghee in the sun, and I should be able to use it. I did so, and was able to move about. I heard that the English had taken the Khyber Pass : when I saw the people fleeing, with their families, I knew it to be true. We heard that the Burra* Sahibs had been taken away to Bameean, and that Akber Kan intended to keep them till his father† was released. I once heard Afghans say that they had lost at Char-ee-kar and Cabul from two thousand to two thousand five hundred men. I don't know what chiefs were killed.

I don't know when Captain Codrington died, or where he was buried. I believe he died the night after he was wounded, but it was kept secret, for fear the men should be dispirited. We were told you said he was alive, and that relief was coming from Cabul. There were four of us in the Khelat-i-Ghilzie Regiment, viz Hunnooman Doobay, Natoo Sonar, Dhurmoo and myself; in the 3rd Hill regiment five. and seven entered the Hill regiment of Pheroo (Ferris:) Saheb.

I heard that when the troops left Char-ee-kar, some went with you. some in another direction, and others with Mr. Rose followed you. I heard that he and Hunnooman Jemadar were killed.

* The English officers.
† Ameer Dost Mahomed Khan

Jyc Deb's wife was with him, she was young; we were often threatened in joke, but no one interfered with us. I don't know who was the owner of the fort near us; it was a musket shot and a half distant from us. I don't know what became of the —— Adhikari. Jye Deb once went to the Barracks, he told me there was nothing there but men's skulls and bones. The stream in front of our Barracks, was half a musket shot distant. I was* fifteen or sixteen days without any water at all. The only food I had after I was wounded, was once some raw mutton and a seer of coarse flour which I had by me; part of it I ate dry. I believe there were about 200 killed and wounded before the retreat. Mohun Beer is in a Ressaleh at Kohat.

Statement of BULLAY SARKIE, *Naik, 1st Goorkha Regiment, 6th Company. Made at Buxa, Bhoolan, 13th January,* 1867.

When about twelve years of age, I was at Cabul with my sister's husband, Sookea Sarkie, Havildar of Shah Schooja's 4th or Ghoorka Regiment, 6th Company. I went with the Regiment by way of Shikarpore in 1838. I was with the regiment at Bameean, Syghan, and at Char-ee-kar.

The night we retreated from that place, I left by the postern gate with my sister's husband and his companions, I was with you.

The 1st, 2nd, 3rd and 4th Companies were formed into a square, and the women and children were placed in the centre; in this manner we started. We soon, however, broke up and were scattered about. At daylight we reached Khoja Serai; there were about 250 men and 16 women. At between 7 and 8 o'clock fighting began. Mr. Rose, and the Quarter Master, Sergeant Hanrahan, and the Soubadar of the 2nd Company were killed. They killed some of the women and seized me and the rest. I remained eleven months in a Shikarpore Khutree's† house. When troops came, I joined them and met you.

You gave me 4 rupees for expenses. I came to India with Nowell Sing, attached to Broadfoot's Sappers. Seven or eight hundred of the enemy surrounded us at Khoja Serai. Only three or four of our party escaped. About 50 were collected from different quarters, and kept at Khoja Serai for two and a half months, then Prince Futteh Jung sent for them, saying he

---

* This statement I have no doubt was made in perfect good faith, we all had lost count of time.

† Hindoo merchant of Shikarpore, in Sind.

would employ them. The Hindoo shopkeepers had supported them
up to that time. They all eventually came to you and served
with Broadfoot's Sappers. I myself saw Mr. Rose killed; they
called upon him to lay down his arms; he threw down his pistol,
whereon they shot him, and afterwards hacked him with their
long knives. The Quarter Master Sergeant was cut down with
their knives, the bodies remained where they fell. Mr. Rose's
dog stayed by his body for ten days; I often called it, but
it would not come away. I do not know what became of it, none
of the bodies were buried.

The fight lasted about an hour; the spot where Mr. Rose was
killed was about two miles on the Cabul side of Khoja Serai.
Our men did not make any stand, they were killed in flight.
Many of the survivors of the Corps are in the Sappers and Miners
at Huftabad (Abbotabad?) The fight lasted fifteen days at Char-
ee-kar.

APPENDIX D.

Extract from the *ENGLISHMAN* Newspaper, of Calcutta,
April 27th, 1842.

Personal narrative of Havildar Motee Ram, *of the Shah's 4th or
Ghoorkha Regiment of Light Infantry, destroyed at Char-ee-kar.*

The 4th Regiment was sent to Char-ee-kar in the month of
May. We were placed in garrison in the guree, then in progress
of erection. Major Pottinger and some other gentlemen were in
another guree, distant about a coss from ours, and called Kalla
Lukman.* To this latter fort we furnished a party of 100 men,
under a Soubadar—this party was relieved weekly. The guree
of Char-ee-kar in which we were placed was quadrangular in
figure, 100 yards long in each face, and having a bastion at each
angle—the ditch from which the earth had been excavated to
build up the walls, at the deepest was only three feet, in other
parts not more than two feet deep. A Khutria, named Hur
Singh, was engaged in building the guree by contract. The
guree of Char-ee-kar is marked A in the accompanying sketch;
there were two gateways to it, with gates, one to the west,
another to the east, marked 1 and 2 in the sketch. At 2 was the

* Killa Lughmanee.

quarter guard of the Regiment, at 1 its rear guard; outside of the gate No. 2 was a number of huts inhabited by the bazar people of the 4th Regiment; in this gateway was placed a long and heavy native gun, 1 should think an eighteen-pounder; on[*] each of the two bastions marked 3 and 4 was placed one of the Shah's six-pounders. A small thread of water was conducted from the neighbouring hills, and a hollow formed from working up the earth with water to raise the walls of the guree; after the flow of water into this hollow was stopped by the Afghans, there continued stagnant in it about fifteen mussucks, vide No. 5. There were no guns on the bastions marked 6 and 7. 1 have shown how all the artillery we had—the three guns already mentioned—were disposed of. The huts for the Sepoys were arranged along the interior sides of the guree, connected together and flat-roofed. There is no water within the fort of Char-ee-kar, which stands on a plain, no hills approaching it nearer than four miles. Our officers' quarters were at the westward gate. In front of the eastern face of Char-ee-kar, and distant from its walls 150 feet, ran a canal B B B, with shelving banks 20 feet in breadth at the top, and about 15 feet deep. The water which ran in it was generally waist deep; this canal was fed by a river to the north, and about six miles distant from Char-ee-kar—the road to Lughman crossed[†] the canal on which there is a bridge—the road is marked S S S S, and to prevent injury to the cultivation, was made to wind considerably to the N. E. of bastion No. 3. About 26 yards off was situated a fakhir's hut and tukeah,—this is marked C in the sketch. To the south of bastion No. 4, distant also some 200 yards, there was an extensive vineyard D; about the same distance, there stood to the S. W. of bastion No. 7 a Musjeed marked E. At F were three tombs of European officers, nearly, I should say, 400 yards from bastion No. 6. G was the target practice butt, distant from, and north of the same bastion, 350 yards. H was a small guree behind the Fakhir's hut, and 500 yards from the fort of Char-ee-kar. The site of the town of Char-ee-kar is marked I I, while K denotes that of the fort of Lughman.

A few days before the Dewallee, Mr. Rattray, who commanded one of the Affghan corps, was lured out from the fort of Lugh-

---

* The bastion nearest the town alone had a gun.—J. C. H.

† There is some confusion of ideas here; the road from Char-ee-kar and Lughman e ran parallel to the canal for about three miles, then crossed the canal at right angles to the castle, distant about 500 yards.—J. C. H.

man by Shah Mahommed of Nijrow, to look, he said, at some recruits which he brought with him for service. They were mounted men. As Lt. Rattray was examining them drawn up in a line, Shah Mahommed gave his troopers a wink, when they wheeled up from the right and left, and enclosed Mr. Rattray, who was shot with a pistol, and his body, which was afterwards recovered, hacked to pieces. I heard this from the Goorkha Moonshee Mohun Peer who accompanied Mr. Rattray, but escaped under the horses' bellies. The men who murdered Mr. Rattray now made a dash a tthe Fort of Lughman. Mr. Rattray's Regiment[*] of Affghans immediately joined the assailants. The attack had continued for the space of two hours, the Affghans being kept at bay by our guard. Capt. Codrington then directed[†] Lieut. Haughton to take the 2d and 8th Companies to re-inforce Lughman. Our men took each 60 rounds of ammunition in their pouches. When they had expended 50 in skirmishing, and killing numbers of the Affghans, they were ordered to close and charge; they did so; a great number of the Affghans sought refuge in a vineyard, but were almost entirely destroyed by the bayonet and cookry.[††] All the Affghans who had been attacking the fort of Lughman drew off, and our two companies returned to that of Char-ee-kar, which they reached at 3 o'clock p.m.[§] A few hours afterwards firing was heard at Lughman — the Affghans were fired upon by our people when endeavouring to remove their head.

The following morning it was observed that the enemy were very numerous about Lughman, and pressing its garrison hard; so[§§] at 6 a.m. the 1st, 3rd, and 6th companies of my Regiment, with a six-pounder drawn by bullocks, under the command of Lieutenant Haughton, issued from the Ghurree Char-ee-kar, with the view of assisting our troops at Lughman. We advanced, until we arrived within half a mile of Lughman, without opposition; at this point a body of 1,000 of the enemy's infantry, with a few horsemen interspersed amongst them, attempted to cut off our way; this party we easily repulsed. We now had arrived at a bridge near Lughman, on (at) which our six-pounder was

* There were only a few horsemen with the Political Agent.—J. C. H.
† It will be seen from my narrative that Motee Ram is mistaken, Captain Codrington being himself shut up in Lughmanee.—J. C. H.
†† The cookry is a Goorkha weapon.
§ This is also a mistake; they did not get back till dark.—J. C. H.
§§ It will be seen from my narrative that Motee Ram was ignorant of the cause for which this party was sent out, and his memory is at fault as to some details.—J. C. H.

placed; suddenly from all quarters a rush was made for the gun by immense multitudes of Affghans, who had concealed them-selves in the vineyards and different buildings round about. It is difficult to form any accurate notion of the number of our assailants so scattered, but it struck me there must have been 25,000—all the villages of Kohistan, Punjsheer, and Gorband poured forth their inhabitants against us; the whole male popu-lation in this quarter of Affghanistan had taken the Ghazi's oath. Our front, rear, and both flanks were attacked simultaneously, but the most serious attack was in front, or from the Lughman side, the plain between which and where we were was completely crowded with Affghans. We repulsed them all with great slaughter, but suffered severe loss ourselves. Lieutenant Salus-bury* was killed—shot in the chest, and placed in one of the two doolies we had with us. The Quarter Master Sergeant was wounded. The Soubadar of my company, the 6th, Singh Beer by name, and a most gallant officer, was put in the second doolie. The Quarter Master Sergeant was able to walk, supported by two sepoys. We had now been absent three hours from the guree of Char-ee-kar, a great part of which time we were seriously en-gaged. It was now observed that heavy bodies of the enemy were against Char-ee-kar itself. We were ordered to retrace our steps; the 1st company was thrown out as skirmishers to cover our retreat; those badly wounded it was impossible to carry off with us, we were so hotly assailed. The Affghans quickly killed them, and seemed to take much delight in mutilating their dead bodies, and pitching their severed members to a distance from each other † We fought our way back to the gurree of Char-ee-kar, which we reached about 10 o'clock a.m. The Affghans now surrounding the fort of Char-ee-kar, and seeking shelter from our fire behind the walls of the vineyard, the target practice butt, officers' tombs, Musjeed and Fakhir's hut, annoyed us very much; it rained bullets. Leaving 200 men in the fort, and tak-ing out the two six-pounders, Captain Codrington drove the enemy from all the positions they had taken up around us. At the second discharge one of the six-pounders§ broke down. The

* The sergeant was wounded in the chest, and sent in on the only dooly we had; Salusbury, mortally wounded, walked half a mile to the barracks, supported by two men. We had but one dooly.—J. C. H.

† This is a pure piece of imagination.—J. C. H.

§ This too is incorrect; the gun broke down while I was firing it, on our retreat. —J. C. H.

Affghans entirely vanished for the present, but the water ceased to run in the canal B B B. We found afterwards that the Affghans had diverted it to the eastward at the point marked L. Our casualties in the whole of this day were very numerous. About 10 o'clock p.m. when the canal had become dry, the enemy appeared again, retaking possession of all their former positions and of the now dry canal besides, the banks of which effectually screened them from our fire.

Towards morning the attack on the fort became more feeble, until at last it ceased altogether; however about 7 o'clock the whole mass of the enemy precipitated itself against the fort; horse and foot leaguered us round on every side. The two six-pounders (we had mended the broken one in the course of the night) were taken out with the greater part of the regiment, while the long gun fired from the gateway on the enemy. One of the six-pounders again broke down; the bulk of the enemy were again beaten off, but a continued skirmishing amongst the the vineyards and different buildings was kept up until night-fall : half the men of the regiment remained in the fort, while half skirmished, and thus relieved each other alternately. At 10 o'clock P. M. Major Pottinger, another gentleman, and the party from Lughman which had been as busy as ourselves, joined us. The want of water began to be felt severely by us; there was scarcely any provision within the fort. We did not mind that so much as the torments of thirst. The enemy continued attacking us daily. On the 3rd day, as well as I can remember, all the Affghans collected in a body to capture the long gun at the gateway; there were whole beeghas of gleaming swords moving towards us, and shouts of a "Chari yar, Alli Mudut" rent the air. We answered them back at every discharge of the long gun, "Gorucknath kejy." This assault was by far the most severe we had yet experienced. Major Pottinger and the other European officers said they never witnessed such a conflict. Capt. Codrington was shot through the chest. He was carried to his quarters alive, but died shortly after. Major Pottinger was wounded in the thigh. We charged the Affghans and drove them in the direction of the point were the water was turned off. On this occasion we partially destroyed the Fakhir's Tukea where we always observed the Affghans clustered thickest. Next day, a seer of water was served out to each man by Lieut. Haughton; this water was obtained from the hollow marked 5 in the sketch. The second day after, half a seer was supplied; in a few days it diminished to a chit-tack, and at last ceased altogether. Some doombahs [sheep] were given to us by the officers; we found relief from sucking the raw flesh, and some of the men placed the contents of the stomach of the sheep in cloths, and wringing them very hard obtained some moisture to assuage their raging thirst. The sick and wounded now increased to a frightful amount, and were continually screaming for water in piercing accents. Our muskets were so foul from incessant use that the balls were forced down with difficulty, although separated from the paper of the cartridge which usually wraps them round. The lips of the men became swollen and bloody, and their tongues clove to their palates.

I ought to have mentioned that the day Capt. Codrington was killed, your old Shikarree* at Lohooghat, Nur Singh, was also slain. He was the best shot among us; every time he fired he killed an Affghan. The European officers were so pleased with him, that he was to have been made a Jemader. Days and nights rolled on. We were continually engaged with the enemy; the men used to steal out in the night to the spring which formerly supplied the hollow marked 5, but which the Affghans turned off in another direction. Those who had the canteens you sent up with the last Goorkha's Levies, used them; those who had lotas only, took them with them covered in clothes, lest the glitter of the metal should lead to detection; those who had neither lotas nor canteens resorted to the use of cloths which they dipped in the fountain and brought back saturated with moisture. When any of these adventurous spirits returned to the fort, all struggled round them to procure one precious drop. The Affghans, however, found out the practice, and shot down all those who approached the spring. For two days there was not a single drop of water within the wall of the fort; the men were mad with thirst, and demanded to be led against any perils to procure water. Accordingly, at midnight, Lieut. Rose† conducted a party of 100 men, taking with them all the lotas and canteens they could carry, and all the bhistees and non-combatants to the spot marked M, where the water from the new cut had overflowed its banks, by the route marked by arrows pointing from the Gurree of Char-ec-kar. Having luxuriated for a short time in the delicious element, and filled our vesssels with it, Lieut. Rose took us to a field of

* "Your old Shikarree" Motee Ram was addressing this narrative to Major McSherry personally.—Ed. "Englishman."

† Ensign A. Rose, 54th N. I.—Ed.

radishes marked N. Here we crammed as many as we could into our mouths and stuck our belts full of more for our comrades in the fort, to which we set out on our retrun by the route indicated by arrows pointing towards it. Shah Mahomed with a body of 3,000 men had taken post at the spot marked O. at an early hour of the night, and erected his standard at P.—A great number of his men were in the now dry bed of the canal B B B.; they seemed to keep a negligent look out. Lieut. Rose said to us, " Give them one volley, then the steel you know to use so well." The non-combatants carrying the water were placed out of harm's way behind a wall. We fired together by word of command from Lieutenant Rose on the slumbering crowd of faces witin 50 yards of them. We then charged shouting " Goruknath ke-jy, " and set the bayonet and cookry to work with a will. A company drawn up in readiness at the gateway to assist us, should we require their aid, heard our battle-cry, rushed down to the canal B B B. extended itself along its banks on the Char-ee-kar fort side, and slew the Afghans as they tried to scramble out on that side. On the opposite we were performing the same operations. Those who had cookries did most execution; there is no weapon like the cookry for a hand-to-hand fight. Mahomed Shah himself was killed, and we captured his green flag, and carried it off in triumph to the fort Char-ee-kar. Shah Mahomed's flag was a very magnificent one; its staff was surmounted by a trident [crescent?] and ball of gold, and the flag itself was six feet long and equally broad, made of the finest green broadcloth, with a figure of the sun splendidly embroidered in the centre. It was an old acquaintance of ours, and changed bearers frequently, as we successively shot them during our long term of fighting. We had somewhat spoiled its beauty too, by piercing it with bullets; the artificial sun shining in the light of the real one, as it waved out in the breeze, offered a famous mark. We were as happy in Char-ee-kar that night as we could be under the heavy loss of our fallen comrades, and in sight of the sufferings of those wounded, who were stretched on the ground thickly around us. The thirst of all* was completely relieved, and their hunger partially so. Our officers were proud of us, and we were proud of ourselves and of each other. The officers said, Shah Mahomed's flag should be ever retained in the regiment as a memorial of that night's achievement. For some days after the capture of Shah Maho-

* That is, all of Motee Ram's party.—J. C. H.

med's flag, and the death of its owner, the enemy relaxed his efforts and we our fire. This interval of comparative repose was most grateful and refreshing to us. The number of Afghans had very perceptibly diminished in our vicinity. Five days* passed when the horrors of thirst began to assail us again. At last a message was received from the treacherous inhabitants of the town of Char-ee-kar that they dared not turn the water down to us themselves, as they would assuredly be murdered, if they did so; but that we might come and throw a dam across the new cut at L., remove the other dam, and cause the water to flow in its wonted channel again. Two hundred men,† accompanied by Lieutenants Haughton and Rose, and taking our fourahs or digging tools with us, proceeded along the banks of the canal B B B to L. On the road we had some skirmishing, but not much. As soon as the men came in sight of the water at L, many of them rushed madly forward, and began to drink; while in the act of doing so, a heavy fire was suddenly opened upon them by the ambushed Afghans in the gardens, houses, and behind the walls of the town of Char-ce-kar—this fire caused great havoc amongst us, and we were forced to retreat without effecting our object. Dying of thirst, lamentably reduced in numbers—weakened by toil and hunger, the Afghans clung more closely round as our exertions in our own defence became less energetic. A mine,§ the shaft of which commencing at the Fukhir's Tukeah C, and passing by Bastion 3, terminated in a chamber at Bastion 4, was sprung. A third of the Bastion 4 was destroyed, two men were buried in its ruins—the dotted line from C to Bastion No 4 shows the course of the shaft of the mine. The Afghans are very expert miners—they learn the art from continually digging "Careezes." The explosion of the mine in question seemed to be the signal for another determined onset on the part of the Afghans. The stock of grape shot originally brought from Cabul had been expended, bags were filled with musket balls, and loaded with these; the heavy gun at each discharge cut long lanes in the throng of Mongelas, while we kept up a continual fire from the roofs of the Barracks The Mussulmans pressed on nevertheless; the party protecting the gun below was annihilated, and the cannon

* There is here such complete confusion of ideas as to time, that I feel it impossible to put the narrative right.—J. C. H.

† This is a mistake, as there were only two digging hoes and two picks with the regiment.—J. C. H.

§ Such a mine was an impossibility: see my account.—J. C. H

almost in the clutches of the enemy, when Lieutenant Haughton
called out, " Down from the walls, every man of you, and rally
round the gun, which is nearly in the hands of the enemy, and
with it go the lives and honour of us all." We every one of us
rushed out of the gateway, and charged the enemy, who recoiled
from the shock as far as the canal B B B, to which they confined
themselves; keeping up a dropping fire on the walls of the
Gurree. We buried this day within the fort the bodies of Capt.
Codrington, L. Salusbury, the Serjeant Major, and upwards of 200
of the Sepoys of the 4th Regiment. The following day the Lohar
Mistree* of the 4th Regiment, who was a native of Hindoostan,
and who served in the regiment from the time it was first raised,
but was a Mussulman and married to an Afghan, wife of Char-
ee-kar, together with the gunners, who were all Mussulmans
from the Punjaub, plotted to leave us, and go over to the enemy.
In attempting to put this into execution, they proceeded to the
gateway, but as they were going out, Lieut. Haughton seized the
jemadar of the Golandauze to detain him ; the latter immediately
drew his sword, cut at Lieut. Haughton, and wounded him in the
hand severely, and breaking loose, Lieut. Haughton called out,
" Shoot these *nimuck harams.*—they are off to the enemy." We
fired at the party as they ran in the direction of the canal, and
dropped five of them. The third day† after this event, our number brought down to a little more than 200 men fit for action,
without water, without foot, and only thirty rounds of ammunition per man remaining, it was determined to evacuate the Gurree
of Char-ee-kar, and endeavour to fight our way to Cabul. At
midnight we moved out; we had only two doolies§ in which were
placed Major Pottinger and Lieut. Haughton, the bearers of all
the others were either killed or had died. Nearly 300 of our
comrades, dead, dying, or so badly wounded as to be unable to
walk, were left behind within the ghurree of Char-ee-kar. I don't
know whether the guns, which were also left behind, were
spiked or not. I think from the death of Lieut. Rattray until the
period of our finally evacuating the Gurree of Char-ee-kar,
twenty-one or twenty-three days must have elapsed. I had too
much to do to take account of time. I cannot give dates, but I

* This man was faithful, and gave me his opinion that the gunners were plot-
ting.—J. C. H.

† Here again Motee Ram is mistaken ; it will be seen that the retreat took place
the very night I was wounded.—J. C. H.

§ There were no doolies ; we rode.—J. C. H.

narrate events in their order of succession, to the best of my memory. I ought to mention that the walls of the Gurree of Char-ee-kar had only reached the height of one cubit above the roof of the Sepoys' Barracks when the fighting began; consequently so low a parapet gave us little protection from the enemy's jazails, which told on us from a distance, one half of which only muskets could carry to with effect. The day after Capt. Codrington's death, to remedy this defect, the officers tore up their tents, and made bags of the canvas, filled them with earth, and placed them on the walls, to cover us from the Afghans' fire.

At the time hostilities broke out, there were two Goorkha Fakhirs in the fort, who were visiting on a pilgrimage the different Hindoo shrines in Afghanistan. They demanded that arms and ammunition should be given to them. Our officers complied with their request, and these sturdy and holy personages astonished us all by their feats in action : there were none of us who fought the Afghans better than they did. We marched on during the night without molestation, until we arrived at a village near Kara Bagh, the second regular marching stage from Canbul on the Char-ee-kar road. Here opposition commenced, and we advanced skirmishing until we reached Kara Bagh, about 3 o'clock A. M., by which time our movements became generally known, and our enemies were getting round us in hopeless numbers every minute. The road ran though the middle of the town of Kara Bagh with walls and vineyards on either side : these the Afghans lined, and from them poured a deadly and frequent fire on us. Numbers were killed—we were totally vanquished; there was a gateway into a vineyard on one side of the road. I rushed through it; an Afghan laid hold of my clothes to detain me, but I shook him off and continued my flight, taking care to carry off my musket with me, for which I had only 5 rounds remaining in my pouch. I ascended the summit of the hills, and ensconced myself in a hollow far up in the mountain, where there was water, during the day—on the coming of night, I endeavoured to make my way to Caubul; I had arrived within two miles of the British Cantonments there—when the dawn discovered to me that I had got into the middle of the Afghan troops besieging the place at the time. I saw at once all hope of further escape was gone. I had 100 rupees in my kummerbund, which sum I amassed in the Shah's service. I took it out and buried it, placing a stone which I thought I could again recognize, over it, and sat down quietly to await what might happen. Shortly a party of horse, about 25 in number, belonging to Hajiz Khan and Bahahdeen approached the spot were I was, and they immediately dismounted—some seized me by the feet, some by the shoulders; one man, taking up my own musket, snapped it three times at me. I am a Mussalman, said I; God does not will that you should kill me—the musket won't go off. The fatalist I addressed threw down the musket, drew his sabre, and with its sharp edge pressing on my throat called on me to say the kalma, else he would immediately sacrifice me. I did repeat the kalma —the sabre was removed from my throat and they carried me to Bahahdeen, first depriving me of my coat, pantaloons, a silk handkerchief, a pistol, my shoes and some other articles, leaving me only a pair of pyjamhs. Bahahdeen gurree is situated I should think about three coss from the city of Cabul. While I remained with Bahahdeen for five days, the people of the village continually threatened to put me to death. Bahahdeen at length released me, giving me an old tattered loonghee for a turban and my own chogah, and saw me a coss on my road. After he left me I had proceeded a coss, when a man ploughing on the road side seized me, and threatened to kill me, unless I worked his plough. I did so until evening, when he took me to his house and there gave me a scanty meal. This man employed me 10 days in guiding his plough. While with him, I suffered severely during the night time—the weather was bitter cold, and I had nothing to cover me but my chogah. I examined the roof of the the house, during the day, and it appeared to me that by removing a few of the bricks from a sort of chimney I might get out unobserved. At night I did so, and effected my escape for the time.

I had got five coss further on the road to Jellalabad, when the son of a sirdar who was fighting at Cabul (I don't know his name), sent some horsemen to take and bring me to him. I was taken to the gurree, all the inmates of which, young and old, male and female, gathered round, exclaiming, "A Kaffir or Feringhee : kill him ; kill him ;" but the young chief protected me from violence, and told me to groom his horse. This young man was continually looking in the direction of Cabul, through a telescope which he said Sir A. Burnes had given his father as a present. I was hard-worked and ill-fed in this family. I remained with them about eight days, when the young chief transferred me to a native of Ghorbund who came to his village, and rented his grazing ground for a large flock of camels. I was employed tending these camels for some twenty days. I was not well fed. I had made acquaintance with a servant of my compulsory master. This servant was a Huzara, who received one rupee two annas a month as wages. He became kindly disposed to me, and one day told me that our master designed to sell me to some Bokhara merchants, with whom he was at that moment driving a bargain about me. I immediately ran away, to escape the intended sale. On crossing the river at Bhoothak, five Affghans seized me, and asked me if I were a Feringhee. I replied in the negative, and stated that I was a discharged camel man of Shah Shooja's; they asked me why Shah Shooja had discharged me. I answered that the King, being mewed up in the Balla Hassar, said he had no employment for camel men at present. Fakeera, my new captor, took me to his house, where I remained some time, hard-worked and ill-fed, as usual. While tending Fakeera's dhoombahs in the jungles, I heard a youth say, "Ukhbar has allowed the Feringhees to depart to-day, and our people are following them from Cabul." When night came on I went to the spot where I had deposited my rupees, and regained possession of them. I set off after the British force, and overtook it at Khoord Cabul, as it was setting out from thence. At Jugdulluck the British force was girded round by Ukhbar Khan's horsemen, who were killing all they could. I extricated myself from this scene of carnage, and sought safety once more in the hill tops. I remained a day high up in the hills. I had tasted no food for twenty-six hours from the time I made my last insufficient meal. I was benumbed by the cold. I could no longer contend with the never-ending dangers and hardships which beset me. I wished for death to release me from sufferings now become intolerable. I descended to the roadside, determined to declare myself to the first Affghans who approached, and court the blow of some pitying sword. I saw a party approach, and concluded the hour of my death had arrived. The party turned out to be five Hindoo Cutries; these Cutries said, "As you are a Hindoo, we will save your life you must pay us for doing so, and to make sure of it we will exact payment beforehand." They then searched me and took the 100 rupees out of my cummerbund, and returned me ten of them—they conducted me to a Dhurmsalah in which there was a Hindoo

Fakhir. His protection I also sought, and gave him my remaining ten rupees. He dressed me up in the red dress of a Fakhir, and rubbed wood ashes over my face. I was to pass for his chela, or disciple; and he said I was to accompany him in the character of such on a pilgrimage he proposed making to Hurdwar. A party of fruit merchants shortly after arrived. The Fakhir, the cutries, and myself joined them. We descended the high road considerably to the left of Peshawar. I begged my way, until I got to Sir Jasper Nicoll's Camp, one march this side of Loodianah.

The sketch I have drawn shows pretty correctly, I am convinced, Char-ee-kar and all it embraces—you had taught me how to make such sketches. You have known me many years, and you know if I ever told you a lie or brought you false information. You will therefore attach such credit to my tale as your appreciation of my character, so familiar to you, may adjudge.

(True translation.)

T. MacSherry, Major, 30th N. I.,
Late Goorkha Recruiting Officer, S. S. F.

Simla, March 31st, 1842.

APPENDIX E.

Narrative of Mohun Beer, *a Moonshee in the employ of Major Eldred Pottinger,* C.B. *The original statement, corrected by Sir R. Shakespear.*

The city of Char-ee-kar in Kohistan is about 46 miles direct north of Cabool. In November, 1841, there was a Cantonment about half a mile north of the city, in which was stationed the 4th Regiment of Shah Shoojah's Infantry (742 strong) and 3 of H M.'s. guns, which with their men had been in the service of Dost Mahomed Khan.

The officers present with the regiment were Captain Codrington, commanding; Lieut. Haughton, Adjutant, Lieut. Salusbury, Quarter Master; and Ensign Rose; there was also a Serjeant Major by name Burns, and a Quarter Master Serjeant named Hanrahan. The fort of Lughmani is about one and a half miles from the Cantonments, and in it resided at the time now alluded to Major E Pottinger, C. B., Political Agent; Lieut. Rattray, Asst. Political Agent, and Mr. Asst. Surgeon. The Fort was a square of about 50 paces,* the walls of mud of considerable thickness and about 60† feet high.

The Cantonment was dependent for its supply of water on a water course; and the destruction of this small force by the Kohistanees appears to have been mainly caused by their having turned off the stream into another channel.

On the morning of 3rd November, 1841, about 9 o'clock, I saw about 3,000 Kohistanees collected round the Fort Lughmani; their chief said, "They are all our people, and we have brought them here to go with Mr. Rattray and fight with Meer Musjadee, near Ak Surai, about 16 miles from Lughmani." Each of them had a gun; some were loaded before they arrived, and some were loading when I saw them; about 17 chiefs were sitting in a tent with Major E. Pottinger and Mr. Rattray in a small garden beyond the Fort. About 1 o'clock P. M. three of the chiefs said to Mr. Rattray, "You must take care and not come out to see people, or they will kill you; they only came here for that purpose, and to take this fort; after which they will attack the Cantonments."

Mr. Rattray said, "They have all eaten our salt, and could never be guilty of such an act." Half an hour afterwards, Mr. Rattray came from the Fort, and told me to come along with him to see these Kohistanees. I accompanied, with his Mirza and a Chuprassie.

When Mr. Rattray came near them, all the chiefs paid their respects to him saying, "Inshallah, we shall go to-morrow and fight with Meer Musjadee." Mr. R. said, "Very good, if you go, I will give you some sowars." Mr. R. then turned to go back to the Fort, but Jubber Khan asked him to look at his men, to which he agreed and turned back again. When he had taken about six or seven steps, one of the Kohistanees called him by name, and ran at him, firing his gun at Mr. Rattray, who turned and ran towards the Fort. I, the Mirza, and the chuprassie all ran towards the Fort. When I had nearly reached it, I looked back and saw Mr. Rattray lying down on the plain. I ran again towards him; and when near him he called me, and told me to take hold of him and help him into the Fort. Directly I took hold of his hand, about

* Really 400 yards.—J. C. H.

† Query, six feet. They were in some places not more than six or seven feet; and at the officers' quarters—the highest point—probably not more than twenty feet high.—J. C. H.

50 Kohistanees fired, and Mr Rattray received a ball in his forehead; I then ran back and got into the Fort, where I found Major E. Pottinger looking towards the Kohistanees and firing at them. About half-past 4 p. m. Adjutant Haughton came to the Fort with two companies, and attacking the Kohistanees, killed 40 or 50, driving the rest towards the hills. Captain Codrington left about 60 sepoys in the Fort, and returned with the remainder to Cantonments.

The next morning (4th November) the Kohistanees collected about twelve or thirteen thousand men on the hills. Lieutenants Salusbury and Haughton came out with two companies and one gun, attacked, defeated, and dispersed the Kohistanees, but Mr. Salusbury was very badly wounded by a gun shot wound in the groin.* When Major E. Pottinger saw the enemy running away, he told me to take 25 sowars and join Lieut. Haughton, which I did. Lieut. Haughton told me to send 12 of the sowars to Mr. Salusbury, and to take 12 to Captain Codrington in Cantonments. When I arrived, Captain Codrington told me to remain, but to send the sowars after the enemy. When Lieut. Haughton and Salusbury had expended all their ammunition, they returned to Cantonment, and during the night Lieutenant Salusbury died.

During the whole of this day we were fighting near Cantonments, and that night the Kohistanees went back to the Fort Lughmani, which they surrounded and began to undermine. There were about 24 hostages, sons of different chiefs, in the Fort, and we had there also 10,000 rupees of treasure. Major Pottinger and the Doctor, with their servants and 60 sepoys, stole out of the fort at night and crept up to Cantonments, where they arrived about 8 o'clock. When the hostages saw our party going away they remained quiet, because they thought that if they made a noise, the Kohistanees would come in and divide the treasure. When the hostages had divided the treasure, they opened the large gate, and called out to the Kohistanees to come in. On entering, all the chiefs exclaimed, " We have beaten them, and to-morrow we will take the Cantonments. "

On the morning of the 6th, Major Pottinger sallied out of the Cantonments with a gun and two companies, and took up a position near a nullah from where he begun to fire at the enemy, but in half an hour he was wounded by a ball in his left foot ; he then took the gun back to Cantonments and left two companies.

*Shot through the back and stomach.—J. C. H.

When Captain Codrington saw that Major Pottinger was wounded, he went out to the two companies, but was very severely wounded by a shot in the back. All his sepoys began to cry for him; we were fighting with them until evening. About 50 or 60 sepoys were wounded this day, during the whole of which we had sufficient water. Captain Codrington was able to walk into Cantonments, but fell down before he reached his house and asked for water; we carried him and laid him on the same bed as Major Pottinger, when he asked for pen, ink and paper, and wrote a letter to his wife whose picture he also gave to Major Pottinger. He lingered on until the night of the 7th, when he died. We buried him and Lieut. Salusbury in one grave. During the night neither our men or the enemy fired.

On the morning of the 6th, the fighting recommenced and continued until evening. That night we had water; on the morning of the 7th, Lieut. Haughton defeated the enemy, and drove them about a mile from Cantonments, and we thought that they would not return any more that day. Serjeant Major Burns was shot in the groin, and died; and a great many sepoys and non-commissioned officers and a Jemadar were killed : we had very little water that night, the enemy remained about one and a half miles from us, and continued firing* at us, and we returned the fire all the night through.

On the morning of the 8th, Lieut. Haughton sallied out with 2 companies, and defeated the enemy and returned to Cantonments with his men. Lieut. Haughton served out the water with his own hands this morning, quarter of a seer to each man. We were fighting until the evening, but at night we had not much firing from the enemy, nor did we fire.

On the 9th, the firing commenced again very sharply ; this day a great many sepoys were killed and wounded; the sepoys had very little water, a quarter of seer to each ; the enemy went to the city of Char-ee-kar that night.

On the morning of the 10th, we had no firing, but in the evening both parties commenced. Ensign Rose went out with two companies and killed about 60 Kohistanees, and brought in water, and one of their standards and three or four matchlocks.

On the morning of the 11th, we had very little firing, and we thought they would now go away and not attack us again. At

* Long shots ! Some mistake here.—J. C. H.

night they fired at us to prevent our getting water. That day the sepoys had not a drop of water, nor until the 14th.

On the morning of the 14th, Major Pottinger,* Lieut. Haughton, Mr. Rose and the Doctor decided on leaving the Cantonments at night, and retreating to Cabool. About 2 p. m. the jemadar of the golandaze heard of the arrangement, and determined to try and save himself by going to the enemy. He rushed on Lieut. Haughton and cut him on the hand with his sword, and then went over with his men to the enemy. About 8 p. m. we quitted Cantonments and commenced our retreat to Cabool. At about 4 miles we came to some water, which the sepoys rushed to drink, and here it was decided† that Major Pottinger and Lieut. Haughton, being both wounded, should ride on in front with me, leaving the regiment to follow behind. Major Pottinger placed Mr. Rose, Quarter Master, and Quarter Master Serjeant Hendrigon§ in charge of the regiment and gave orders to them to come on quickly. When we arrived near Ak Serai, we found a large nullah in which we concealed ourselves all day, we then mounted our horses and rode over the hills, and at 4 a. m. on the 16th we arrived at the Cantonments at Cabool.

(Signed) H. M. LAWRENCE,

A. A. G. G.

* Mohun Beer was Moonshee to Major Pottinger, and naturally mentions him first.—J. C. H.

† I never heard of any such proposition, and certainly would not have consented to leave my men if I had ; besides they were our only protection.—J. C. H.

§ Hanrahan. This is certainly a mistake. Pottinger led the advance. Rose and the Sergeant brought up the rear, being both unwounded ; the Sergeant's wound had healed.—J. C. H.

www.ingramcontent.com/pod-product-compliance
Lightning Source LLC
Chambersburg PA
CBHW022151090426
42742CB00010B/1467